Someone once said that getting there is half the fun. Someone else also said, "Hey, that new ship, the *Titanic* — it's unsinkable!" That shows we can't depend on what someone once said.

So says Emmy-award winning comedy writer Gene Perret as he reflects on the humorous hazards of travel in *Someday I Want to Go to All the Places My Luggage Has Been.* Here are more of his insights:

ON ERRANT DRIVERS:

You're allowed to get three questions wrong on your written test and still get a driver's license. On the freeway, I sometimes glance over at the guy driving alongside me at 70 miles an hour and wonder which three he got wrong.

ON BAGGAGE CHECK-IN:

A man was checking in for his flight to St. Louis. "Do you have any luggage to check?" the clerk asked.

"Yes, I have three pieces," the man said. "I'd like this large one to go to San Francisco. The tan piece I'd like sent to Peoria, and the green suitcase should be delivered to Albuquerque."

The clerk said, "Wait a minute. We can't do that."

The man said, "Why not? You did it last week when I flew to Pittsburgh."

ON FLYING WITH KIDS:

The church requires three miracles before a person can be considered for sainthood. In the modern era, though, three trips on an airplane with a toddler next to you — or near you — is an acceptable substitution.

D0181900

To

My Little Petunia

WͥtWorks™

A funny little division of Arizona Highways Books

2039 West Lewis Avenue, Phoenix, Arizona 85009.
Telephone: (602) 712-2200   Website: www.witworksbooks.com

Publisher — Win Holden
Managing Editor — Bob Albano
Associate Editor — Evelyn Howell
Art Director — Mary Winkelman Velgos
Photography Director — Peter Ensenberger
Production Director — Cindy Mackey

Library of Congress Catalog Number — 99-62103
ISBN — 1-893860-01-9

SOMEDAY I WANT TO GO TO ALL THE PLACES MY LUGGAGE HAS BEEN
First edition published in 2000. Printed in the United States.
Book Designer — Mary Winkelman Velgos

Gene Perret

SOMEDAY I WANT TO GO TO ALL THE PLACES MY LUGGAGE HAS BEEN

Cover Illustration by
James R. Shepherd

WịtWorks™

CONTENTS

What is travel? Very simply, it's getting from where you are to where you want to be. At least, that's what it was at the beginning. Nowadays, it's getting from where you are to where you want to be . . . with a three-hour layover in Chicago. But originally it was getting from here to there.

Someone once said that getting there is half the fun. Someone else also said, "Hey, that new ship the *Titanic* — it's unsinkable!" That just shows us that we can't depend on what someone once said.

Early humans had no use for travel. They had no irresistible urge to ski in Vail, sun themselves on the Côte d'Azur, or squander their weekly paycheck on a weekend in Atlantic City. Because they didn't know those places were there . . . if they were at that time.

Prehistoric man didn't know about travel. He was "here." "Here" was where he wanted to stay. He didn't want to go "there" because he didn't know "there" was there. We've found no fossils of prehistoric bus terminals or train stations. They didn't need them. They wouldn't have turned a profit. Prehistoric man was happy where he was. "Here."

Travel then was unnecessary. There were nice caves in the area so they set up communities in them. They raised their families in these caverns. They were content. But when an 80-foot dinosaur with paws as big as a pickup truck and teeth the size of trees came stomping through their villages foraging for edibles, they probably turned to one another and said, "I think this would be a good time to get away from the neighborhood for a while."

Travel was born.

The first travel, of course, was by foot. That's a misnomer. It should have been called "travel by feet." You're not going to cover much ground using just one foot. However, that's what the terminology is, so we'll live with it.

That first form of travel was slow, tiring, and dangerous, but you didn't need a reservation. You just went, so in a sense it was convenient. You journeyed by day, rested by night, and killed animals for nourishment along the way. It was primitive and inconvenient, but on the other hand, the food was generally better than what's available with most current forms of travel.

Eventually, horses were used to get from here to there. It was just like going by foot except that you used someone else's feet. It was much easier so it became very commonplace. They even had frequent traveler awards. They were called saddle sores.

The next step was to hitch a wagon to the horses. Now people could really move. They could throw all their belongings in the back of a covered wagon, toss the kids in the back, paint "California or Bust" on the side, and really go from here to way out there.

Of course, this form of travel had drawbacks, too. Those drawbacks would swoop down from the hills and shoot arrows at your wagon. You would be on a very relaxing part of your journey when suddenly you'd hear, "This is your wagon master speaking. We're about to be attacked by a band of marauding warriors. Please remain calm, return your buckboard seats to their upright and locked positions, and move the wagons into a circle." So the travelers would naturally obey those commands, just as today we obey the command to remain seated "until we come to a complete stop at the terminal, and the captain has turned off the seat belt sign." Those pioneers would put the wagons in a circle.

That probably could have been improved on, too. Arranging the wagons in a circle just made it easier for the renegades to ride around and shoot arrows at them. If they had had the ingenuity to position the wagons in a square, many of the warriors would have fallen off their horses trying to make the turns.

Nevertheless, that's hindsight. They chose to fight from a circular barricade. It must have been a very distressing layover in one's travel plans. I can imagine the head of the household firing at the attackers and cursing the bad luck. "Why did we have to take this route through hostile territory? Why did they have to pick this wagon train to attack?" And his spouse would say to him, "Oh, c'mon now, Pa. Don't be a grouchy face. You know what they say — 'Getting there is half the fun.'"

Another offshoot of this was the stagecoach. This was what you took when the local gunfighter told you to get out of town or else. You either got on the noon stagecoach, or you didn't. If you didn't, then the next form of transportation you would use would be pallbearers.

Then came the horseless carriage, the automobile. That got you where you wanted to be faster than walking or riding a horse or carriage, but never fast enough to satisfy the kids in the backseat, who kept saying, "Are we there yet?"

For a long time, the train was the most popular form of travel in the nation. Then it dwindled down to just something for Johnny Cash to sing about.

Airplanes replaced it. In December of 1903, the Wright brothers revolutionized travel forever. They successfully flew for the first time a heavier-than-air mechanically powered craft. It was amazing how accurately that first flight foreshadowed modern air travel. For instance, there were two brothers, Orville and Wilbur, and only one seat. The very first scheduled flight was overbooked and Orville was bumped. The plane flew 120 feet in

12 seconds over a field in Kitty Hawk, North Carolina, but somehow Wilbur's luggage ended up in Fargo, North Dakota. Also, they didn't have enough honey-roasted peanuts to go around, and they were out of the meal that Wilbur had selected.

That's how we got where we are today — ready to taxi out for takeoff with a book about all sorts of travel adventures. So fasten your safety belts; put your seatbacks in their upright, locked, and most uncomfortable position; return all your carry-on bags to the overhead bin or under the seat in front of you; and sit back and relax with some of the inconveniences of getting from where you are to where you want to be.

TRAVEL IN GENERAL

*Life would be so much
easier if all of us would just
stay in our rooms.*

THE TRAVELING TOO MUCH TEST

Communication is so easy today. We not only have telephones, but we have conference calls and video phones. We have fax machines and e-mail for instant communication. Still, companies insist on face-to-face meetings, sales pitches, and the like.

Business people travel incessantly.

I traveled quite a bit and relished it as a status symbol. Then I found out that they sent me on so many excursions simply because neither my boss nor my co-workers liked having me around that much.

You may be leading the same sort of nomadic life, packing and unpacking suitcases, trying to remember which room you're in in which hotel. In fact, you may be traveling too much for your company.

Here's how to tell if you are.

You know you're traveling too much for the company when:

You look in the mirror one day and notice that your ears are beginning to resemble luggage tags.

You greet your wife and children on your arrival home and you notice that they're all wearing name tags.

You develop a bad back because your spine keeps wanting to

return to its full, upright, and locked position.

You go to an elegant restaurant and complain because your silverware didn't come wrapped in plastic.

Your wife says she's having your favorite meal and you think she's talking about honey-roasted peanuts.

Your spouse brings you a cocktail and you check to see if you have the exact change.

Your spouse says she wants to do anything to make you feel comfortable and you ask for a complimentary deck of cards.

Before starting your car, you stand up, face your passengers, and point out to them where the exits are.

You sit down to a nice home-cooked meal and you're startled at the first bite because it tastes like food.

Your legs feel awkward your first few hours at home because you have a place to put them.

You make out your will and leave each of your loved ones just enough to be comfortably stowed beneath the seat in front of them or in the overhead bin.

Every time you go out to pick up the morning paper, you bring your boarding pass with you for re-entry.

You drive home from the airport and instead of pulling into your driveway, out of force of habit, you circle the block for 20 minutes trying to find a better parking space.

You return the sofa you just bought to the furniture store because you discover that the cushions on it cannot be used as flotation devices.

You arrive home from the airport and the family requires two forms of picture ID before it lets you into the house.

You hesitate before going through any doorway for fear you might set off the metal detector.

You drive to work and find yourself waiting for the captain to tell you what's out your left-hand window.

Children ride in your family car and you invite them forward to look at the driver's seat.

You park your car in the garage, but instead of going into the house, you look around for signs leading to the baggage claim area.

Instead of telling your spouse you're leaving to go to work, you say, "Sweetheart, I'm about to de-house."

As soon as your car turns into your driveway, you stand up so you can be the first one off.

You paint the curb outside your house white for "loading and unloading only."

You walk into your own house and look around for the check-in counter.

As the song suggests, our world is filled with "far away places with strange-sounding names." Each of these places has an intrigue and beauty all its own. Unfortunately, the name doesn't always share that intrigue and beauty. For a traveler, these strange-sounding names can be embarrassing and confusing.

As an example of embarrassment, suppose you are journeying to a place called "Pig Holler." You don't want to stand at the front of a line of world-traveling executives and say, "One ticket to Pig Holler, please." It would probably be less humiliating to simply fly into Coyote Canyon (a nearby community) and hitchhike to Pig Holler.

Now you may wonder how that could be less embarrassing. Don't you still have to tell the driver where you want to go? Not really.

The driver stops and says, "Sure, hop in."

You do.

He asks, "Where you going?"

You say, "Are you going as far as Muskrat Valley?"

He says, "Yep."

You say, "Well, I'll hop off in the town right before that."

You can do that with a driver who picks up hitchhikers. You can't do that with commercial airline pilots.

As an example of how strange-sounding names can be confusing, consider the poor tourist who wanted to fly from Los Angeles to Oakland, cities in the same state, a flight of less than two hours. After more than five hours in the air, the traveler finally asked the flight attendant when they expected to land.

She told him, "Oh, we have another seven hours before we touch down in Auckland." Auckland, not Oakland. That's in New Zealand, not northern California.

Strange-sounding names can be confusing.

There is a town in the southwestern part of Arizona named "Why." Picture yourself buying an airline ticket to go there.

"I'd like to buy a round-trip ticket, please. I want to go to Why."

"Where?"

"Why."

"Because I have to know where you're going."

"Why."

"To know how to issue the ticket, I have to know where you're going."

"Why."

"Because you can't get on the plane without a ticket, and you can't get a ticket unless you tell me where you're going."

"Why."

"Is there some reason why you can't tell me where you're going?"

"Why."

"That's what I'm asking you. Now tell me where you're going."

"Why."

"That does it," the clerk says, picking up the phone and calling security.

"Please send an officer over to ticket desk 34 immediately."

Now, see, that makes sense. They give each desk a number. There's no embarrassment, no confusion. The security people know exactly where ticket desk 34 is. It's between ticket desks 33 and 35 . . . probably. Airports don't call their ticket desks silly names like we do our towns and cities. There's no ticket desk "Why," or ticket desk "Pig Holler," or ticket desk "Skunk Mountain," or any such confusing names. They're all simply numbers.

We should have done that with our countries, states, counties, cities, and towns. Consider the example above and how much simpler it would have been if Why, Arizona, were simply 3690524.

"I'd like to buy a round-trip ticket, please. I want to go to 3690524."

"You've got it, sir. Here's your ticket. Have a nice flight."

Wasn't that easy?

We should drop the names of all places and instead issue them numbers. It would be easier and much less embarrassing. Of course, it would take some of the romance out of a few of our treasured songs, like "Moon over 8733421" or "In the Blue Ridge Mountains of 7644213." And the long-running Broadway play "Oklahoma" might have been "654338921." The title song would start:

(Sing along if you like.)

Siiiiiix — 54338921, where the wind comes sweeping through the plains. . . .

And end with:

We're only saying, "You're doing fine 654338921. 654338921 — 6-5. . . .

Admittedly, it's a bit awkward. It doesn't scan too well and it certainly doesn't rhyme, but there's much less confusion.

It is a little late to start making this change, as beneficial as it obviously would be. There's too much pride involved now. Texans are proud to call themselves Texans. It wouldn't be as much fun for them to say, "Yessir, I'm a 59832149-an and proud of it." And the same applies to folks who are just as honored to be from other states and towns.

The idea is impractical now. It should have been initiated at the beginning — with Adam and Eve. They lived in the Garden of Eden. They should have lived in 1. That would have started the number thing rolling. Then when they were expelled, it would have continued.

"Who are you?" Adam says.

"I'm an angel. I've been sent here to banish you from 1."

See, there's another fringe benefit of numbers over names. There's less emotional attachment. To be banished from the Garden of Eden is upsetting, traumatic, disastrous. But if you're exiled from 1 — big deal.

"What do you mean?" Eve says.

The angel answers, "You can no longer live here in 1."

Adam reponds, "But we like 1."

The angel says, "You should have thought of that before you decided you like apples, too."

Eve says, "And for that we're being tossed out of 1?"

"Exactly," the angel replies.

"Where will we go?" asks Adam.

"2," says the angel.

"Suppose we don't like 2?" Eve asks.

"Then move to 3."

"And if we don't like 3?" Eve persists.

"Move to 4."

Adam says, "And if we don't care for 4, I suppose we move to 5?"

"Good guess, Adam," the angel says. "You could very well be the smartest man on Earth."

Adam says, "And suppose we keep moving and we work our way all the way up to 999,999,999 and we don't like any of them. What then?"

"Well, then I guess you could just go to the devil," the angel says.

No, the angel wouldn't say that.

But the angel, under our present system, might just say, "Well, then you could go to this little town in the southwest corner of Arizona."

Adam would say, "Why?"

And the angel would say, "Oh, you know the place?"

And the confusion would have started all over again.

IF WE COULD TRAVEL
LIKE THE MOVIE STARS

They say that art imitates life. I wish it did, especially when it comes to traveling. Travel in the movies and on TV is antiseptic. It's painless and stress free. Not so in the world you and I live in.

For instance, anyone who gets around by car in the entertainment world always finds a parking space — immediately. And it's right in front of wherever he's going.

I watched a film last week. The movie lasted two hours and, in that time, the star found eight parking spaces, all directly in front of his destination. I drove around for two hours and 18 minutes trying to find a parking space to go to see this movie. When I finally did find a spot, it was nowhere near the movie house. In fact, I finally parked and walked to the theater, and on the way, I passed my house.

Art imitates life, indeed.

Also, I love it when movie stars are driving somewhere and they want to get the latest news. They click on the radio and immediately get a news report talking about whatever they wanted to hear. I click on the radio and get rap music, then country and western music, then some talk show host babbling on about school lunch programs, then four or five foreign language stations and then a heated political discussion. No way do I ever hear what I want.

Even airline travel is convenient for movie people. If they're in a hurry to get to the airport, they raise their hand, shout "Taxi," and a cab pulls over. They get in and they're off to catch their plane. If you and I ever tried that, we'd better be sure to have a fully refundable ticket because we would not make that flight. We might not even get there the day of the flight.

When the movie people do get to the airport, the cab pulls right over and drops them conveniently at the curb outside of their terminal. Normal people get to the airport and the curbside is packed. Buses are fighting to pull out in front of our vehicle. Other cars pull into available spaces before we can get to them. Finally, in desperation, we jump out about three lanes from the terminal with traffic zooming by us on both sides. We risk our lives trying to get ourselves and our luggage safely on the pavement. Movie people don't.

Even when movie stars land, they get a cab right away. Often, they're pursuing someone and they jump into a cab and say, "Follow that car." The driver does. I've never had occasion to ask a cab driver to "Follow that car." I hope I never do. If I did, though, it would not be as easy as it is in the movies. But for the movie star, the cabbie just follows orders. He's at an airport with five or six lanes jammed with traffic. Hundreds of cars, taxis, and shuttle buses are zooming by. Yet he obediently "follows that car." Just once, I'd like to see him turn to the star of the film and say, "Which car?" Never would happen.

When movie people reach their destination, they hand a bill to the driver and rush off. They never ask how much. The driver never even checks what they give him. It's just a done deal. The camera follows the star as he rushes to his next plot point, and the cab driver motors off. Sometime I think the camera should follow the cabbie. Then as he gets about four or five miles away, he would look at the bill and exclaim, "Hey, that guy gave me a $5 bill and the meter read $24.20."

No one ever asks, "How much?" in movies. They pay the cabbie, they buy their airline tickets, they order food at restaurants. They don't care what it costs. It's different for you and me. We want to know what the damages are. Film people don't care. When you're paying with theatrical money, price is no object.

In airports, movie stars walk right up to the counter and buy their tickets. No hassle, no bother. In real life, I make my reservations weeks ahead of time, and when I get to the terminal to check in, I wind up in a line that snakes back and forth three or four times before it reaches the clerk. I have a 20-minute wait, shuffling my luggage a few feet along every three minutes or so. When I finally reach the next-in-line position, I invariably get behind a businessman who is making a tour of 128 American cities and 14 Canadian ones. He wants to change his connections and assigned seat on every flight. That never happens in the movies.

The hotel rooms in movies astound me. Folks check in and their room is larger than my home. They have room to pace. They have a table on which to enjoy their room-service meal. My hotel room is of the vaudeville variety. You know, the kind about which some comedian said that he had to go out to the corridor to change his mind. The sort of room about which Fred Allen said, "My room was so small even the mice were hunchbacked."

Even cowboys in Westerns traveled more conveniently during frontier days than we must today. Cowpokes would ride into a strange town, walk into a saloon they've never been in before, and order "whiskey." They would gulp down the shot, slam a coin on the bar, and leave. They didn't ask, "How much?" They didn't wait for change. They didn't have the hassle of the barkeep saying, "Hey, I don't have change for a gold piece. Don't you have anything smaller?" None of that.

And if they planned to stay awhile instead of drinking and running, they would say, "Leave the bottle." Try that in some of the finer restaurants in your town. In fact, try it in a local dive and see if you get away with it.

It's not debatable. If you want problem-free travel, forget hunting around for a reliable travel agent. Become a movie star instead.

IDEAL LUGGAGE

The Lone Ranger never rode off without Tonto galloping alongside him. Don Quixote always had Sancho Panza aiding him as he thrust his lance fiercely toward offending windmills. Bud Abbot would never step into the spotlight without the comfort of Lou Costello at his elbow. You and I are the same. We never journey anywhere without a piece of luggage tagging along.

The difference, though, is that the Lone Ranger probably liked Tonto. Don Quixote must have felt some affection for Sancho Panza. Abbott was friendly toward Costello. I hate my luggage.

Surely, you've seen or heard of those ads where a gorilla is playing with a brand-name suitcase. The ape tosses it around the cage, stomps on it, punches it, squeezes it. That's what I'd like to do with my valise. Or better yet, I'd like to hire an orangutan to do it for me.

While you are traveling, luggage is something that slows you down and tires you out. In short, it's a nuisance. Yet we need it to go anywhere. Unlike the birds of the air and the lilies of the fields, we can't function without an occasional change of drawers. Hence, we need the suitcase.

Luggage manufacturers are trying to make our luggage less unwieldy and more of a traveling companion than an encumbrance. For airline travel, they've invented under-the-seat bags, none of which fit under the seat. They've created "expandable" cases. They're reasonably sized for a normal amount of contents, but none of us travels with a "normal" amount of contents in our bags. Consequently, we always use them in expandable mode, which makes them resemble hogs fattened for the kill.

Nothing the good-intentioned manufacturers do seems to work. So, I've taken the job on myself. Here's my design of the ideal piece of luggage:

The luggage when empty should weigh absolutely nothing. When fully packed, it should weigh even less. That may be a difficult requirement to meet, but with today's space-age technology, manufacturers should be able to find an anti-gravity material of some sort. If not, then they shouldn't be in the luggage business in the first place.

Naturally, the luggage should have wheels. Even though it's lighter than air (provided the manufacturers have paid diligent attention to item 1) it's still undignified nowadays to carry baggage. It should be led through the airport like a well-behaved dog. But the important part of item 2 is that the suitcase should have a sense of balance. I don't know, do it with gyroscopes or electronic stabilizers — I don't really care how. It should not teeter and totter and waggle and wobble and fall over every time it passes over a slight bump in the pavement. It should hug the road as it follows behind you.

Each piece of luggage should be assertive. When

you deplane and hustle through the terminal to the baggage claim area, your suitcase should be working on your behalf. It should brashly and confidently elbow its way past other valises and duffel bags so that when the handlers finally give the OK for the luggage to slide onto the carousel, yours is the first one down the chute.

Each individual piece of luggage must come off the assembly line with its own unique color. No two suitcases should be allowed, by law, to be the same color or even similar in tone. Each piece should be readily identifiable from a distance. This is so that when you do see your bag winding toward you on the baggage carousel, you won't whoop and holler. You won't jump up and down and shout, "There it is. There it is," only to find out when you pull it from the carousel that it belongs to Wendell Frelbish from Ocotillo, Arizona. It's not your suitcase at all. That's not only disappointing, it's embarrassing and it should not be allowed. If bags were all manufactured in distinctive colors, it wouldn't happen.

The suitcases also should be equipped with a robotic voice, you know, similar to the voice in cars that tells you to "fasten your seatbelts," "turn off your headlights," and such. It's a technology that already exists. It should simply be incorporated into luggage. One phrase would be used for those people who come on the airplane late with tons more baggage than they should be allowed to carry on. They open and shut overhead bins searching for one inch of space so they can cram in their folding garment bags right on top of your carefully arranged luggage. When these people open the bin, your suitcase should be programmed to say in a firm, if robotic sounding, voice, "Shut the door and get outta here."

Another phrase would be activated when the suitcase goes through the metal detectors as you go into the boarding area of the airport. It should say, "The guy behind me looks suspicious. Why don't you get him to open his bags?" Then while they detain that passenger for what he thinks is a random inspection, you can be leisurely walking to your gate, dragging your lighter-than-air, technologically balanced valise behind you.

A good utilitarian suitcase should be self-closing. You simply pack it — cram it, even — with all that you'll need for this trip. Stuff as much as you want in there. When you're finished, turn and face the wall, cover your eyes and count to 100. When you turn back around, your suitcase is closed and latched. You don't need a family member to come sit on it. You don't have to kneel on it and force the latches shut. It does all that for you.

Oh, and I almost forgot. The suitcase should have a secret entrance to it. Why? Well, because we all stuff the suitcase, shut it, set it upright, then let out a sigh of relief, saying, "Well, I'm finally packed for this trip." Then we remember something we forgot to pack. Now we have to set the suitcase on top of the bed again, open it, step back while it pops open because it's so crammed full of things we won't need, put in the almost-forgotten item, and close it again. Not with the modern suitcase. Now you can just slip it through the secret entrance. No fuss, no bother.

We want this suitcase to be part valise, part valet. No matter how much you squeeze into it, when you unpack, each item is neatly pressed and immediately wearable.

This luggage should also be round-trip friendly. No matter how loaded that bag is when you begin your journey, it will always have room for the junk you pick up and must tote home. Don't ask how the manufacturers are going to do it, but we all know they must.

Finally, the luggage should be priced under $30.

There they have it. The challenge has been issued to the luggage makers. Create that suitcase and I'll buy it immediately. Well, maybe not immediately. I might wait until they have a sale.

TRAVEL IN THE GOOD OLD DAYS

I enjoy watching Western movies. Many people do. Some like to root for the good guys in the white hats. Others get emotionally involved and want to see justice done. Many love the suspense of wondering if the cavalry will arrive in time. Me, I just get envious. Traveling was so much easier in the Old West.

When cowpokes would ride into town, they'd head for the saloon, the hotel, the general store, the sheriff's office. Wherever they wanted to go, they always found a parking space. Well, actually a hitching space. But there was always room for one more horse. They never had to circle the block three or four times waiting for some other cowpuncher to back out. No sir, there was always room for their horse at that particular hitching post.

And it was free. You never saw a cowboy fumbling for change for the parking meter, or hanging a sign on his stallion that read, "I went in to the general store to get change for a $20 gold piece.

Please don't give me a ticket." They didn't need that sort of nonsense. There was parking available, and one didn't need change to take advantage of it.

Then when the cowboy walked into the saloon after a rough ride, he didn't have to stand there beside a dumb sign that said, "Please wait to be seated." You and I do. We stop at a lunch-eonette and even though there are seats all over the place, we can't take any. We have to wait until someone tells us which seat to take. Restaurant employees pass us by, but no one offers to seat us. Why should anybody? There's a sign there that says, "Please wait to be seated," so they're going to make us wait.

Citizens of the Old West didn't have that problem. The cowpuncher just walked into the local saloon and sidled up to the bar. You try to do that today and some employee will chase after you. "Hey, no sidling. Can't you read? Wait to be seated." So we wait.

The most convenient part, though, was when the bartender approached the cowboy and said, "What'll it be?" The cowboy would say, "Whiskey, and leave the bottle." Isn't that nice? How easy can it get? Wouldn't you love to walk into a cafeteria and say, "Coffee, and leave the pot," or "Gimme a glass of milk, and leave the cow?" How about, "I want a dry martini — straight up — and leave the olives." It doesn't happen that way today.

Paying for everything was so easy in those Western films. The cowboy would simply reach into his vest pocket, slam a coin onto the bar, and walk away. I tried that once at a cafeteria and the manager chased me out to the parking lot, yelling, "Hey, pal."

I turned and said, "What?"

He said, "Your check came to $14.22 and you left just a quarter on the counter."

I paid him while trying to explain that back in the Western

towns you could pay by leaving just a coin. He counted the money out as he walked back into his restaurant while muttering something about having public hangings in the Old West, too.

Getting a hotel room was less complicated in frontier days, too. You didn't need a reservation or a confirmation number. The cowpuncher just walked up to the clerk and said, "I need a room."

The clerk said, "Sign the register."

The cowboy signed, and the clerk said, "Pay in advance."

The Westerner reached into his pocket, pulled out a coin and slapped it on the desk. See, everything in the Old West cost the same thing — whatever you had in your vest pocket. It never cost any more and you never got any change. It's much more complicated today.

And nowadays, we always have to ask how to get to our room. "Go down this corridor past the gift shop, the lounge, and the arcade with all the noisy games in it. Then, turn left and go down the corridor past the banquet rooms. You'll see the elevators on your right. Take one up to the third floor and cross over the covered walkway to the Tower Building. Go past the Gourmet Restaurant, which opens at 5 P.M. but you'll need reservations, and take the Tower elevator up to the seventh floor. Your room is overlooking the pool on the right side of the corridor."

In the Old West, the room was easy to find. It was always at the top of the stairs.

The clerk would say, "You're in room 3. It's at the top of the stairs."

Or the clerk would say, "You're in room 9. It's at the top of the stairs."

Or the clerk would say, "You're in room 1427A. It's at the top of the stairs."

It was always at the top of the stairs.

If there weren't any stairs, it wasn't a hotel. Then you had to ask someone, "Where can I get a room for the night?"

That someone would say, "Martha's boarding house, right at the end of town. Tell them I sent you and they'll give you room 6. It's at the top of the stairs."

Though some aspects of wandering the Old West make modern travelers covetous, you might argue that journeying by stagecoach was slow, dusty, and most uncomfortable. It was. However, it also had features that today's travelers can envy.

The stage pulled into town; you got on. That was it. No metal detectors to go through. No sitting in a waiting area while some stagecoach employee announced, "We'll begin boarding our stagecoach to Kansas City in just a few moments. We'll be boarding by row number. Please wait till your row number is called. Meanwhile, those traveling first class, those with small children, and those who have been wounded in gunfights and may need some assistance in boarding, may board at their leisure."

You didn't have to watch the privileged get on while you patiently waited for your row number to be called. Then you didn't have to sit and listen to that same employee say, "We're now boarding row 1," and you sat there with a ticket that read, "row 2." You didn't have those problems.

You didn't have to worry about finding a spot on the stage-coach for your luggage. The driver tossed it on top with every-one else's, and there was plenty of room for it.

Once you got comfortable in your assigned seat, and the driver had wet his whistle at the local saloon and paid for his drink with whatever he had in his vest pocket, you were under way. It was that easy.

You never had the stagecoach driver turn to you and say, "We're gonna be delayed about a half hour or so, folks. It seems they're having a spell of bad weather in Chicago so they're going to keep us sitting here for a little while."

Those things just never happened in the good old days, when travel was easy. On the other hand, you rarely got honey-roasted peanuts when you rode with Wells Fargo.

A CRUISE,
THE PERFECT VACATION — ALMOST

Cruising is a specialized form of travel. It's elegant. The officers of the ship look so dignified in their neatly pressed white uniforms. The passengers dress tastefully for dinner. At least one night each week, they even don gowns and dinner jackets for formal dining. Elegant.

Airline travelers used to be refined. I can recall when I wouldn't dare show up at the gate without a shirt, tie, and jacket. Today many of the passengers don't wear shoes.

I admire elegance. I don't have it, but I like being around it.

Cruising is appealing for other reasons.

Ships are isolated, removed, islands with a rudder. They're self-contained. A ship is your hotel, your restaurant, your playground, and your vacation spot all rolled into one prepaid package. Not only do you not need to go anywhere else, but you can't. That, to me, is ultimate relaxation.

When I get up in the morning on ship at sea, I'm fairly certain that's where I'll spend the rest of my day. That's a vacation to me.

My spouse, though, is different. If we decide on, plan, and purchase a vacation at Point A, my wife wants to go to Point B.

"Let's go for a drive today, dear."

I say, "I don't go on vacation to drive somewhere else. I want to sit and do nothing."

She says, "Sit behind a steering wheel and do nothing. That's called driving."

I say, "We're here. Let's enjoy here."

She says, "But it's a shame to be this close and not see it."

I say, "If we wanted to see Point B, we should have gone to Point B."

She says, "Then we would have missed Point A."

But we really wouldn't have, because if we had gone to Point B, she would have wanted to leave there and drive to Point A.

That's why I like cruises. If you look at a ship carefully, from every angle, you'll notice that they're all built without driveways.

I like that.

I'm basically a dead head, a do-nothing guy. I'd just as soon watch a ball game on TV as go to the park. In fact, I'd rather sleep through the game than actually watch it.

My wife complains that traveling with me is like carrying an extra piece of luggage. I'm that much fun and that much dead weight. She's right; I admit it. Except on cruises. On board ship, I'm Mr. Activity.

"Hey, honey, let's get going. We'll be late for bingo."

"Sweetheart, I've signed both of us up for the ping-pong tournament."

"Dear, when we get back from the midnight dance, let's figure out what we're going to do for tomorrow's amateur show."

"Darling, have you written your campaign speech yet? I'm running for Honorary Mayor of the ship, you know."

I sign up for every activity and show up with bells on for each party. Do you know why? Because I've already paid for it, that's why.

I just go and go and go.

My wife says, "Don't you think you'd better rest up a bit?"

I say, "I can rest at home."

She says, "Don't I know it."

I say, "Besides, I can rest at home for free. Everything here is already paid for." Then I do a few loosening-up exercises while getting prepared for the 2 A.M. limbo contest.

You see, the cruise already cost X dollars, no matter what we do. If I get involved in everything on board, it averages out to $3.49 per activity. Cruising is a bargain.

The food is an enticement, too. I don't know whether you know it or not, but everything on a cruise ship is edible. Draperies, lamps, tables, chairs — all edible. Anything you see on board the ship, you can eat.

They serve meals constantly. There are breakfast, lunch and dinner, of course. There are also a brunch, an afternoon snack, a late-night snack, a midnight snack, a between-snacks buffet, and a between-buffets snack. If you get hungry at any other time, just call your room steward and order whatever you want. You can literally go from the time you get up in the morning until you climb back under the covers at night and never stop chewing. In fact, the blankets are edible.

The food is great on cruises.

Also, every place you visit on a cruise is interesting. All the dull places are inland.

For so very many reasons, cruising is the greatest vacation in existence. If, though, you're prone to motion sickness, forget everything I've said.

CHAPTER TWO

TRAVEL AND THE FAMILY

*Whoever said that getting there was
half the fun never had to travel
with my family
in the back of the station wagon.*

VACATION ALTERCATION

My family and I have differing philosophies about vacations. To me, a vacation is a time to relax, rejuvenate, and have some fun. To my kids, it's a time to find fault with whatever country, state, city, resort, and room we happen to be in. Nothing suits them. One daughter even complained about the ocean.

She was toweling herself after a splash in the surf and I asked her, "How's the water?"

She said, "Needs more salt."

Not even the Atlantic Ocean pleased her.

It seems as though the whining escalates in proportion to how much the excursion costs.

We went to Hawaii one year. Before we left, I called a family meeting and announced to my four youngsters — ages 8 to 12 — that Mommy and I would be spending a lot of money, but it was for a good cause. We wanted to relax and have fun together. I also suggested to the kids that they each bring along a little bit of their own cash.

If they wanted to buy some silly, useless souvenir, they didn't have to get Mom and Dad's permission. If there was something they wanted to do, they didn't have to come to us for the cash. They could just do it. They agreed it was a good idea, and they all brought along a few bucks.

Our first night there, I treated the entire family to an elegant dinner. It was my "Let's get this vacation off to a rousing start" treat. The rest of the 10 days would be hot dogs on the beach and fast-food restaurants that fit into our budget.

The vacation didn't get off to a rousing start. Quite the opposite. During the meal, one daughter was a total grouch. She didn't like the ambience, the food, the waiter. In fact, she wasn't crazy about the rest of us being at her table, either. Her foul mood spread. Soon, brother fought with sister, who fought with the other sister, and so on.

I had to put a stop to this because I've learned from experience that hotels and restaurants absolutely refuse to give part of the money back when you don't have a good time. I've tried and they're adamant.

When we got back to our suite, I called another family meeting. Family meetings excite me because they give the illusion that I'm in charge.

I asked the grouchy daughter what the problem was. She said, fighting back tears, "I lost $5."

"Honey, that's a pity," I said, "but look on the bright side. Mom and Dad are paying for this vacation. We're paying for your airfare, your room, all the things we do together. You've got a vacation that's worth more than $1,000. Don't you think it's silly to throw it away for five?"

She said, "It wasn't your five bucks." Then she ran off to her room in a huff and slammed the door.

None of the enticing travel brochures had pictures of a family feud on them. This family, I determined, would have a good time whether it enjoyed it or not. Still thinking I had the meeting under control, I asked the rest of the family what they thought. They were very frank.

They said, "You were a bit harsh with her. After all, it wasn't your $5."

In an effort to salvage this vacation, I took a $10 bill out of my pocket. Like a stage magician, I passed it around so they could all verify that it was genuine. Then I took some matches from my pocket. With a flourish, I set fire to it. It burned for awhile in my hand, bringing gasps from everyone, especially my wife. Then I set it down into an ashtray, the bill turned to a small black ember, and tiny flakes floated around the room.

"There," I said, "now Daddy has lost $10. Can we all forget about the money and simply enjoy each other's company and have fun on this trip?"

Just then, my daughter came running out of her room waving a bill over her head and shouting joyously, "Hey Dad, I found my $5!"

I was a total grouch for the next 10 days.

ARE WE THERE YET?

I'm going to do it. Someday I swear I'm going to do it.

I'm going to write out a check and rent the house at the corner of our street.

My wife will say, "Why would you do that?"

I'll say, "For our vacation this year."

"Our vacation?" she'll say.

"Our vacation," I'll restate.

"Why would you pay out good money to rent a vacation house on the corner of the street where we already live?"

I'll tell her, "Because every year, we select someplace new for our vacation — the mountains, the lake, the seaside resort. We cram the car with all of our paraphernalia. We load the kids in the back. And we take off for a restful holiday."

"So?" my wife will say.

"So," I'll go on, "every year, we get to the corner of the street and one of the kids will invariably whine, 'Are we there yet, Daddy?' So, one of these years, I'm going to pull the car over, park, and say, 'Yes, we're there,' and get out and spend our two-week vacation in the house at the corner of our street."

Just for spite I'm going to do it. Someday I swear I'm going to do it.

TRAVELER'S CHECKLIST

It doesn't matter how many places you've visited, how frequently you travel, or how far you go, you can never leave the house without that little voice inside you whispering, "Haven't you forgotten something?"

That little voice inside me is often augmented by the real voice coming from the person sitting next to me in the car. Every time my wife and I begin a motor trip, we go through a checklist like a pilot and co-pilot of an airplane.

She usually begins with the basic necessities. "Have you got your pills?" she asks.

"Yes."

"Money?"

"Yes."

"Underwear?"

"Of course I have underwear."

She says, "I don't mean are you wearing underwear. I mean have you packed underwear?"

I say, "Boy, I forget to pack my BVDs one time, and I'll never live that down, will I?"

She says, "Well, it made for a very unpleasant Alaskan cruise."

"Well, I'm sorry," I say.

She goes on. "Underwear is one thing they don't normally sell on a ship."

"I know, dear."

"And it's not something you can easily borrow from fellow travelers."

"I know, dear."

She adds, "You found that out, didn't you?"

"Yes I did, dear. And I packed underwear for this trip."

"Are you sure?"

"I'm absolutely positive."

"Just checking."

We drive in silence for awhile. My wife is trying to think of other things I may have forgotten, and I am silently trying to recall whether I really did pack underwear.

"Toiletries," my wife shouts with no warning.

It startles me. "What?"

"Toiletries. Shaving cream, razors, after-shave lotion."

I say, "Honey, I have a full beard."

She says, "I know, but why?"

I say, "I prefer a beard."

She asks, "Are you sure it's not because on one of these trips you forgot to pack your toiletries and to this day you're too conceited to admit it?"

We drive silently for several more miles.

"Dress shirts," she says.

"Yes."

"Handkerchiefs."

"Packed 'em."

"Comfortable shoes."

I say, "All my shoes are comfortable. You're the one that has to remember them."

"Well, I did remember them."

"Good," I say.

She asks, "Did you bring the confirmation for the hotel?"

"It's in my briefcase," I say. "How about you? Did you bring a good book to read?"

"Of course," she says. "But I'll bet you didn't bring swimming trunks."

"I did," I say. "I remember packing them right by my underwear." I don't really remember packing them right by my underwear. I just say that to give her the impression that I really did remember to pack underwear.

"Keys to get back into the house?" she asks.

"They're attached to my car keys," I remind her.

"Your phone book in case we have to call someone?"

"In my briefcase," I say.

"Did you bring traveler's checks?"

"In my briefcase."

"Did you bring something to work on? You're always complaining that you're bored on vacation and you wish you had brought something you could work on."

"I did. It's in my briefcase."

"Did you bring your briefcase?" she asks.

I knew she was going to ask that question, and I have my answer ready for her. It's an answer I love because it totally destroys all the other replies. I say, "I think so."

"You *think* so?" she shouts.

"Yeah, I think I put it in the trunk." I know I put it in the trunk. I am just being mischievous.

"Don't you think we should pull over and check the trunk?"

I say, "Honey, I have my briefcase. Relax."

We drive silently again. My wife fumes because she doesn't think my playful little joke was funny.

Suddenly she breaks the silence. "I know what we forgot."

"What?" I ask.

"I know what we forgot," she repeats it as if to impress upon me that saying it more than once indicates that this is serious and not to be kidded about.

"What did we forget?"

"I know what we forgot."

"What?" I demand.

"The tickets. We forgot the tickets."

I say, "Honey, we're driving there."

"Oh yeah. I forgot."

Now this is becoming abnormal, compulsive, obsessive behavior. I reassure my spouse. "Sweetheart, we have everything we need. We packed clothing, medicine, money . . . everything."

"Underwear?"

"Yes, underwear. We have packed everything for this trip except the kitchen sink, believe me."

She says, "Oh my, no. Turn the car around."

I say, "What?"

She insists. "Turn the car around."

I say "We have everything. The kitchen sink is only a figure of speech."

"But we have to go back."

I say, "Why?"

She says, "I think I left the water running in the kitchen sink."

We have to drive back, but it doesn't bother me. While my wife is checking the water that she might have left running, I sneak upstairs to check in our bedroom. I'm not at all sure that I packed underwear.

HAVE YOUR PHONE CALL MY PHONE

Travel once was like meditation. You did it silently, peacefully, in solitude. When you drove along the highway, no one could reach you. As you sat in your assigned seat on the plane, there was no one to talk to except yourself, your seatmate, or your God, asking Him to let the plane land safely. Not anymore. Cell phones have ruined everything.

You see people walking through airports with the cell phone attached to their ear. You hear people at the next table in a restaurant closing a deal with someone halfway across the country. Parents who should be watching soccer games are talking with their brokers via the mobile phone. I fully expect to see accident victims being transported to the waiting ambulance with a brace holding their head still and a cell phone medically attached to the ear.

I hate cell phones. That's why I bought one — in self-defense. No, actually, I bought two. One is for my wife. Having a cell phone is like taking a self-defense class. You're now hoping that someone attacks you so you can get a chance to use it.

My wife and I were on a trip. I had a meeting to attend and she was going to go shopping and meet a friend for lunch. I would join them later after my meeting. Aha! A chance to use our cell phones wisely.

"Leave your phone on," I said. "If the meeting lets out early, I'll call you and arrange to meet you somewhere."

She said, "I don't want to leave my phone on all that time. It's a terrible waste of money."

I said, "It doesn't cost money. You don't get charged unless someone calls you."

"You're going to call me," she said.

"Of course I am. That's why we got the phones."

"Well, tell me when you're going to call me and I'll turn the phone on then."

I said, "If I knew when I was going to call you, I wouldn't have to call you."

"Good," she said. "Then I won't have to turn the phone on."

"Look," I said. "Trust me. Just leave the phone on and I'll call."

"Okay," she agreed.

We hadn't really used the phones yet, so I thought we should test them. "Turn your phone on now," I said, "and I'll call you."

"Why are you going to call me?" she asked. "I'm standing right here."

"I want to test the phones. Pretend you're far away."

She shrugged and turned the phone on.

I said, "What's your number?"

She said, "If I'm far away, how can I tell you my number?"

I said, "You're not far away. You're right here."

"Then why are you calling me?"

"Just give me your phone number, please."

She did.

I dialed her number. Nothing happened.

"What happened?" I said.

She said, "Absolutely nothing."

I said, "What did I do wrong?"

She said, "How do I know? I'm far away."

I said, "I pushed the speed dial on my phone and your phone didn't ring. I don't get it."

She said, "Did you put in the area code when you programmed it in there?"

I said, "No."

She said, "There's your problem."

I said, "We both have the same area code."

She said, "But we're not home now. You have to dial 1, then the area code, then the number."

I dialed 1, then the area code, then her number. Nothing happened.

"Now what happened?" I asked.

"Nothing again."

"Why?"

She said, "Did you unlock your phone for roaming?"

I said, "I don't know what that is or how to do it."

"Get your instruction book," she told me.

I got the book. She flipped the pages, pushed a few numbers, held the phone up to her ear and said, "OK, now you can dial long distance."

"What did you do?" I wanted to know.

"I'll explain it later," she said.

So again, I dialed 1, the area code, and her number.

Her phone rang. It actually rang. She held her phone to her ear and said, "Hello." She sounded as though she were standing right next to me.

I said, "It sounds like you're standing right next to me."

She said, "I am standing right next to you."

She moved away from me and spoke into the phone. I heard nothing.

"I can't hear you," I said.

"Speak up," I said. "I can't hear you at all."

Finally, I could hear her.

"I can hear you now," I shouted jubilantly.

She said, "That's because I'm standing right next to you again. I hung up the phone."

"But why couldn't I hear you? You could hear me."

My wife explained, "That's because I know what I'm doing and you have absolutely no idea."

She was right. She took my phone and instruction book and did some sort of manipulations. "You have to turn the volume up," she explained as she handed my phone back to me.

"Let's try it again," I said.

We did and it worked beautifully. I felt like Alexander Graham Bell must have felt the first time he heard Mr. Watson's voice over his new device.

"OK," I said. "When the meeting's over, I'll call you. We'll arrange for a time and a place to meet."

"Wonderful," my wife said. "But just in case we miss each other, why don't we meet at the corner of 5th and Main at 3 o'-clock."

We met at the corner of 5th and Main at 3 o'clock. I had my instruction book in hand, and my wife had the patience of a saint as she explained to me again what I had done wrong.

GIFT SHOPS

Water used to be an essential part of travel. It was a necessary part of life. Pioneers planned their day's travel by how long it would take to reach the next river or water hole.

"We must push on," the trail boss would say. "The cattle need water." And so they pushed on.

"We'll camp here for the night," the head of the family would say. "It's close to the river."

Stagecoach drivers didn't stop along the route for the comfort or convenience of the passengers. The horses needed water for sustenance and to cool their weary muscles. If the passengers wanted to grab a bite to eat, stretch their aching legs, and tug on their creeping undergarments, that was fine. But they stopped for water for the non-paying critters.

Today, of course, water is no problem. Each traveler carries his or her own bottle. No longer do we have to reach the water hole by nightfall. We've all got a plastic bottle, a portable water hole, clutched in our hands. We've even got slung across our shoulder little containers that hold the bottle on our hips. That leaves our hands free to manage the five or six pieces of luggage that we carry onto the plane even though we're permitted only two. Struggling with all that baggage makes one thirsty. So we squash our bags into the overhead bin, sit down in our uncomfortable seat, and have a sip of water from our squirt tube container.

No, water is no longer a problem. There's no need today to travel from river to stream to water hole. Today's travelers journey instead from gift shop to gift shop to gift shop.

Years ago on a trek across the continent, the worst thing a traveler could hear was "the river's run dry." Today the worst thing I hear on any journey is "Let's stop in this gift shop."

My wife said, "Let's stop in this gift shop."

I asked, "Why?"

She said, "Because it's here."

I said, "Why don't we go hike up a mountain?"

She said, "Because the mountain is there; the gift shop is here."

I made a sarcastic facial expression accompanied by a scornful grunt.

My spouse countered with logic. "When we're at the mountain, we'll hike up the mountain. When we're at the gift shop, we'll go in and shop around."

But as we were walking into the gift shop, I said, "We never get to the mountain because we're always busy looking around in different gift shops."

My wife picked up some trinket and said, "This is cute."

"It was just as cute when we saw it in the gift shop on the corner that we stopped by five minutes ago," I remarked.

"Did they have this there?" she asked.

I said, "They have it everywhere. That particular item is in every gift store in the United States. It's also in every gift shop in Lithuania, Liechtenstein, Luxembourg, and every other country, principality, and province in the known world."

She gave me a look that said, "Who pulled your seat belt too tight?" Then she put the trinket down, saying, "Well, I still think it's cute."

I said, "If you think it's cute, buy it. Then we can get out of the gift shops and do some real sight-seeing."

Then she gave me a different look that said, "I think your brain is suffering from jet lag." She said aloud to me, "Why would I buy it here?"

I was afraid to answer because it occurred to me that any answer I gave would be lamebrained. So I said, "Why not?"

She condescendingly replied, "Because it might be cheaper down the street."

This response hit me like a left jab to the jaw, a right hook into the belly, and then a left cross to the side of the head. It meant we would be going to another gift shop down the street, then back to this one, and possibly to the one I carelessly mentioned that we stopped in earlier. For the rest of this entire day, I was going to be looking at souvenir spoons, ceramic thimbles, and tee shirts with witty sayings on them.

We shuttled back and forth from this gift shop to the previous one. We also searched for gift shops that might be further down the block or on the next street or around the next corner. We picked up items, we priced items, we called each other over from another part of the store and said, "Look at that. Isn't that cute?"

Me, I just tagged along, but my wife shopped in earnest. I was like her caddy, carrying the bag and occasionally offering advice.

My wife said, "Do you think Chuck would like this?" "Wouldn't this look darling in Emily's house?" "Isn't this perfect for little Evaline?" "Wouldn't Martha just adore this?"

My answer to all the queries was, "Yeah."

I wanted to escape from the gift shops. I wanted to get out and see the spacious skies, the purple mountain's majesty, the amber waves of grain, the fruited plains. But no, my wife still had to purchase salt and pepper shakers, to select napkin rings, and to choose the right size of clothing with the punchline "And all I got was this lousy tee shirt" written on it.

I wanted to purchase a shirt that had the saying, "I spent a fortune on this vacation and all I got to see were some lousy gift shops."

And it's true. We missed the morning tour because we had to pick up something for the grandchildren. We skipped the afternoon tour so we could do some shopping. We missed the evening party because if we didn't pick up the gifts during that time, the stores would be closed. As I signed the credit card receipt at the checkout, it dawned on me that I could have seen as much if I had stayed home, and it would have been cheaper, in the long run, to pay to let our relatives and friends come here and pick up their own mementos.

It would have been far less boring for me, as well.

"All right, let's go over this list," my wife said.

I chuckled to myself. I've traveled all over the world. I've taken plane, train, and car trips and it was never any big deal. I'd pack what I needed, check that I had my tickets, pet the dog, kiss my wife and kids goodbye, and be on my way.

My wife, though, when she's about to go out of town, makes a giant production of her exodus. She presents me with a detailed — and I mean *detailed* — list of things I'm to do while she's away.

"I don't have to go over any list," I assured her.

"I'd feel better if you did," she said.

"I'm a grown man," I said.

"I know that," she said. "And that's why I've made a long list."

"Sweetheart," I said, "when I go on a journey, I don't write out a set of instructions for you, do I?"

She said, "That's because when you go away, you leave a responsible, dependable person here to take care of things."

"Right," I said.

She said, "I don't have that luxury."

I pointed out, "I'm here."

"We don't have time to repeat ourselves," she said.

"I hope I can survive without your charming sarcasm around the house," I said.

She pointed to the first page of her "while I'm away" instructions. "I've left a detailed set of directions for watering the houseplants."

I chuckled again; I couldn't help myself. "Honey, I'm a fairly successful businessman. I have over 250 people under my supervision."

She wasn't impressed. "Yes, but they all water themselves. If they didn't, you'd have 250 employees drawing medical benefits because most of them would be suffering from dry rot."

She had a point, so I read over her detailed botanical directives and nodded that I understood them all and would execute them faithfully.

She harrumphed. I hate it when spouses harrumph . . . especially when they have good reason to.

"Now let's talk about the dog," my wife said.

I laughed again. I said, "This is ironic. You have three-quarters of a page on how, what, and when to feed the mutt, but not one sentence on how to feed me."

"The dog can't whip out a credit card and go to a nearby restaurant," she said.

She had a point again.

"Should we have a quick trial run?" she asked.

"What is this? Like the Department of Motor Vehicles where I have to pass a test to stay home alone? I know how to feed a dog."

She said, "I just want to be very explicit because the last time I went away, it cost a fortune to feed the puppy."

"What are you talking about?" I asked.

She said, "The $4.75 long-distance phone call asking where we keep the can opener."

I said, "I never called and asked you that."

She said, "No, the dog did."

I said, "Very funny. Now, why don't you just tell me exactly where the can opener is."

She said, "It's on my instructions, but it's in the top drawer in the kitchen right next to the sink."

I added, "And to put your mind at ease, I do know where the kitchen and the sink are."

She said, "Of course, you do. That's where you store all your dirty dishes and silverware until my return."

I said, "You know, I thought I was going to miss you, but

you're taking care of that well."

She said, "Just be sure to bring in the newspaper and the mail each morning."

I said, "No, I thought I'd get an easy chair and sit out on the lawn and read them rather than lug all that stuff into the house."

"Just remember to do it," she warned.

"I will," I promised.

She said, "I'm going to call you every night to make sure you're following orders and taking care of things."

I said, "Fine. If 911 answers, hang up."

She harrumphed again. I hated it again.

"C'mon, I'll get the car loaded for you," I said. I picked up her luggage, carried it out to the driveway, and loaded it into the trunk.

"Have you got everything you need?" I asked.

Another harrumph.

"Well, I was just checking," I said.

As she slipped behind the steering wheel, I said, "I have some instructions for you, too."

"Oh, really? And what are they?"

I said, "Have a good time and don't worry about anything here."

She said, "I will and I'll try."

Then she drove off.

I missed her even before she made the right-hand turn at the corner of our street. I watched as the car disappeared and wished that she were here with me now. I wanted her here not only because she's a caring, considerate, and efficient wife. Not just because she's got a great sense of humor and is fun to be with. Not only because she's great company and our home is big and lonely without her. But also because I realized I had locked myself out of the house.

CHAPTER THREE

PREPARING TO TRAVEL

*My wife always packs more than I do
even when she's just dropping me off
at the airport.*

THE PRICE IS ALMOST RIGHT

Most of us who have had at least a high school education have studied logic at some time or another. You remember the class. It's where you get a series of three statements and you have to determine logically whether the last statement is true. For instance, (1) all animals have cells (2) all horses are animals, therefore (3) all horses have cells. Obviously, that last statement is true. But here's another example: (1) all horses have four legs (2) all horses are animals, therefore (3) all animals have four legs. That statement is not necessarily true, because the first two statements don't logically prove it.

I know, it's no more fun here than it was in class. The point I'm making is that all those people who passed this class went on to become many different things — doctors, lawyers, butchers, bakers, insurance salesmen, entertainers — many different occupations. The people who failed this class all went on to become the people who price tickets for airlines.

Witness my experience:

"Good morning, thank you for calling Air Anonymous. This is Bridget. How may I help you?"

I said, "Good morning, Bridget. I'm calling to purchase two tickets to Baltimore."

Bridget said, "Fine, sir, and when will you be going?"

I said, "We'll be leaving on April 20."

"That's this year?" Bridget asked.

"Yes," I said.

Bridget told me, "That's a Tuesday."

I said, "That's right. And we'll be returning on Friday the 23rd."

"That's a Friday," Bridget informed me.

"Yes," I said.

"Will you be staying over the weekend?" Bridget asked.

"Not unless St. Gregory changes his calender between now and then," I said, lightening the conversation with a touch of airline-ticket-buying humor. Bridget didn't seem any lighter.

"Will you be traveling together?" Bridget wanted to know.

I said, "Yes. My wife carries my reading glasses in her purse and I hate to change planes every time I want to work on a cross-word puzzle."

More ticket-buying humor. Same response from Bridget.

"I have two seats together in row 18. One is a window seat and the other isn't. Is that all right?"

I said, "Yes." I was going to say that I'd prefer two seats together with both of them being window seats, but I opted against that. Bridget could endure only so much hilarity.

Bridget said, "All right, then, that'll be seats 18A and 18B."

"That's fine," I said. "How much are they?"

Bridget said, "Seat 18A is $245.88 and seat 18B is $310.96."

I figured Bridget was retaliating with some airline-ticket-buying humor of her own, so I politely chuckled and said, "Really, how much are they?"

She said, "Seat 18A is $245.88 and seat 18B is $310.96."

I said, "You're not kidding, are you?"

She said, "Sir, we don't kid on this job."

I should have suspected that from her response to my attempted humor.

I said, "May I ask you a few questions?"

She said, "Of course."

I said, "These seats, they're both on the inside of the plane, aren't they?"

Bridget said, "Yes."

I asked, "And they're right next to one another, right?"

"Right," Bridget said.

"And they both land in Baltimore?"

"Yes, sir."

"At the same time?"

"Certainly."

I asked, "One doesn't come with a parachute or anything like that, right?"

Bridget said, "Sir, they are exactly the same."

I said, "Bridget, $245.88 and $310.96 are not exactly the same. There's about $65 worth of difference in there."

Bridget said, "I realize that, sir, but the accommodations are exactly the same."

"I see," I said. "Bridget, then, let me ask one more thing. This may seem like a dumb question, but why is there $65 worth of difference?"

Bridget said, "Sir, that's an Air Anonymous internal decision. You have no reason to know that."

I said, "Bridget, I have 65 good reasons why I want to know that."

"It's quite complicated," Bridget warned me.

"I'm a reasonably intelligent person," I told Bridget, although I doubt that at this point she believed me.

Bridget said, "We assign x number of seats to be sold at a certain price, x number of seats are sold at another price, x number of seats are assigned to frequent flyers, and x number go to special-priced customers. It just so happens that you've called when we've had only one more seat available at the $245.88 price, so I'm willing to sell that to you if you book your reservation now. The next available seat, therefore, will cost you $310.96 since all of the $245.88 seats are sold out."

I said, "That makes perfect sense to me, Bridget."

"I'm glad, sir," Bridget said.

But I hadn't completed the thought. So I did now. "That makes perfect sense, Bridget, to someone who has been driving nails with their forehead since birth."

Bridget now realized she had a semi-irate customer, so she said, "That's all we have available, sir. Would you like to reserve those seats, or not?"

I needed the seats so I said, "Yes, I'll take those seats. However, I want the less expensive seat ticketed to my wife and the more expensive one ticketed to me."

Bridget said, "Sir, the accommodations are identical. Why would that make any difference to you?"

I asked, "Why did it make any difference to Air Anonymous?"

Bridget wasn't in the mood for a debate so she clicked some buttons on her keyboard, I heard some whirring and clacking in the background, and then Bridget said, "All right, sir, you've got seats 18A and 18B reserved for Tuesday, April 20 for a direct flight to Baltimore, Maryland, returning on Friday, April 23."

"And that doesn't include the weekend?" I asked. I just wanted to get in some sarcasm for the $65 plus I was being gouged.

"That doesn't include a weekend," Bridget said with obvious corporate restraint.

"And seat 18A is the cheaper seat?" I asked.

"Yes."

"And that is booked in my wife's name?"

"Sir, why is that so important to you?"

Here's a company that's charging $65 for two adjacent seats

51

and it's questioning my logic. I said, "Because my ticket will be reimbursed. My wife's will not. Therefore, I save $65 by purchasing the less expensive ticket in her name."

"Then it worked out well for you," she said.

Only an airline that had someone flunk a logic course and charge another 65 bucks for a seat that's going to the same place on the same plane with the same accommodations could reason that it was doing me a favor.

I said, "Bridget, then we are confirmed?"

"Yes," she said.

"I have one more question. If my wife and I decide to change places somewhere over the Grand Canyon or thereabouts, does she then owe me money?"

Bridget hung up.

We flew to Baltimore together. During the flight, my wife asked the attendant for a deck of Air Anonymous playing cards and got them. For pure spite, I asked for a deck also. The attendant told me that was the last deck she had.

And she gave that deck to the cheaper seat. Go figure.

IF YOU'RE GOING TO LOSE MY LUGGAGE, DO IT BEFORE I PACK

Packing is a chore. No, it's an ordeal. No, it's hell. I absolutely hate it and put it off till the last minute. This scene has played out at our house many times:

"Have you packed for your trip yet?" my wife asked.

"No, I haven't," I said.

"Are you going to pack?" she asked.

"Of course I'm going to pack. I can't very well go on a trip without a change of clothes, can I?"

"When do you plan on packing?" she asked.

"I don't know," I responded with a soupçon of irritation. "I'll pack when I'm in the mood to pack. What is this fascination with my luggage all of a sudden? Why are you asking about packing now?"

"Because the shuttle driver is at the door waiting to take you to the airport," she said.

That's how much I hate packing.

The first problem I have with packing is that I carefully plan my journey and anticipate how much clothing I'll need. I bring just the right amount of apparel for the trip — not too much and not too little. Then as I begin packing, my suitcase overrules me. It says, "You're bringing too much."

And my wife always sides with the luggage.

"You're bringing too many clothes," she says.

"No I'm not. I'm bringing exactly what I need," I insist.

"Okay," she says. "You're the one who's going to have to make the trip carrying an open suitcase because there's no way in the world you're going to close that one."

Since it is now two against one, I have to decide which articles of clothing "I absolutely need for my trip" I will put back into the drawers from which they absolutely came.

Shoes are a major problem. You know why? Because shoes can't be folded. They have to go into the suitcase life-size. It's the same as carrying a pair of extra feet in your luggage. They take up precious room.

If someone wanted to make a fortune, that person would invent a pair of universal shoes. You could wear them for travel and to play golf in. You'd wear these same shoes for your roadside jogging, tennis playing, and lounging about. These universal shoes would also look great with your tuxedo for the President's

Ball on Thursday evening.

You'd never have to carry extra shoes with you. I tell you, invent these shoes and you'd make a fortune. I'd buy, well, one pair. What would I need two pairs for? So, maybe you wouldn't make that much of a fortune, but you'd do the traveling world a great service.

On the other hand, I like shoes precisely because they can't be folded. I have a problem folding things that aren't already folded. I'm not even real good, though, with things that are already folded. My wife and daughters can hold a sweater by the shoulders in front of them. Then with a twist of the fingers and a rolling of the wrists, the sweater, in that one move, is neatly folded and ready to pack. It looks just like it came from the store. If I hold a sweater before me and attempt the same thing, I wind up with a lump of cashmere and two very sore fingers.

But women can fold things quickly, neatly, and effortlessly. It comes from years of attending baby and bridal showers and oohing and aahing over all the pretty clothes. Notice that when women see clothing in a box, they are compelled to take it out and hold it up so that they can all ooh and aah more freely. Then they do that finger and wrist thing and it's back in the box as if it had never been removed.

A man will never take clothing out of the box. He might lift a corner of the collar or make some equally tentative move, but he'll never take it out of the box. I know I never will. Once I take a piece of clothing out of the gift box, I either have to wear it or sell it. I'll never get it back in the box.

And I can't get unfolded clothing neatly into a suitcase, either. So my wife folds all my clothing for packing — for a fee.

I don't enjoy unpacking, either. Unpacking implies that I will have to repack again sometime, probably for the trip home. So when I get to my room at the hotel, I open my suitcase and try to take out what I need without disturbing what I don't yet need. I try to slip a handkerchief out without disturbing the nicely folded sports shirts and trousers. My socks don't have to match my outfit. I just reach into the bag, feel around, and slip out the first pair that my fingers find. If they're brown, they're brown. If they're blue, they're blue. It's OK. Even if one's brown and one's blue, that's OK, too.

This ploy never works, of course. Something will snag and pull a sweater out. Once the sweater is out, it's out. There's no way I'll ever get it folded and back in its assigned spot. So I have to wear it.

"Why are you wearing that sweater on such a hot day?" an acquaintance asks.

"I have to wear it."

"Why?"

"Because it came out of my suitcase."

"You shouldn't be wearing that in this weather. It's too hot for that sweater."

"Do you want to buy it?" I ask.

He doesn't.

Also, when my wife travels, she buys a little memento for everyone — kids, grandkids, acquaintances, people we haven't met yet but may meet soon. I buy nothing for anyone because if I do, I'll have to pack it.

My wife always chides me when I come back from business trips. "You should have bought something for the kids."

I say, "If the kids want a memento from Cincinnati, let them come to Cincinnati. I'll gladly buy them something and they can carry it home themselves."

I hate packing that much.

I spent a delightful six days in Surprise, Arizona, with my older sister, Sarah, her husband, Bud, and their teenage son, Chick. We enjoyed telling stories that we've told and heard hundreds of times before. We played countless games of Scrabble, and we enjoyed cocktails and conversations until the yawns became overpowering and some sensible soul said, "I have to go to bed."

"I won't hear of you taking the shuttle," my sister said when it came time for me to leave. "We'll drive you to the airport."

"That's not necessary, sis," I said.

"We insist, pal," Bud insisted. "We don't get to see you that often so we want to spend as much time as possible with you."

So, they drove me to the airport.

"You can just drop me off at the curb," I said when we arrived.

"No we won't," Sarah said. "I want to make sure my little brother gets safely on the plane."

So Sarah, Bud, and little Chick walked with me through the terminal, through the metal detectors, and up to my gate, where the sign read, "Flight 42, delayed."

"Guys," I said, "you don't have to stay."

"Yes, we do," they all agreed.

"But it could be forever. Go on home."

Sarah said, "I'm not leaving my little brother alone in a big old airport."

Bud said, "We can sit and have a drink and enjoy your company all the longer."

Even little Chick said, "I want to stay. You're not only my favorite uncle but the best Scrabble player I've ever seen."

Bud said, "Yeah, what was that one big word you had the other night?

I said, "Quixotical."

Chick said, "That was great. You used all seven tiles and got 'triple word score' three times."

Sarah added, "You got more than 320 points on one word. It's the biggest Scrabble score I ever saw."

After the plane was delayed a half hour, I said, "Why don't you guys go home?"

Sarah said, "I want to make sure you get on that plane."

After an hour, I said, "There's really no reason for you to stay."

Bud said, "Hey, we want to do it."

After two hours, I said, "I'll be fine. Go home."

Chick said, "Yeah, why don't we, Mom?"

Sarah said, "We're staying until your uncle's flight takes off."

"But I'll miss soccer practice," Chick said.

I said, "Sarah, don't make the boy miss his practice."

Sarah said, "It's not going to kill him to sit here for a few more minutes. It's the least he can do after I sat up every night this week playing that stupid game with you people."

I was stunned. I said, "I thought you enjoyed Scrabble."

She said, "I hate that dumb game. That's why I want to get you on that plane, so I can have one night of peace without worrying what kind of word I can make when I don't have any vowels."

I said, "But I really thought. . . ."

Bud interrupted, "Don't pay any attention to her, pal. She really enjoys playing the game. She just doesn't like to play with cheaters."

"What cheaters?" I asked.

"C'mon, pal, you know what cheaters. There's no such word as 'quixotical.'"

"There is so," I said.

"There is not," he said. "I looked it up."

"Where did you look it up, Dad?" Chick asked.

"Under 'K,' where else?" Bud said.

Sarah said, "See? That's what I hate about playing Scrabble. I have to play with people who can't spell."

"I can spell," Bud said.

"Sure he can," Sarah said to me. "His real name is John, but he changed it to Bud because it's one less letter to remember."

I went to the ticket counter and found out the plane would probably be delayed another hour or so.

I came back to my sister and her family and said, "Go home, please."

"Why are you so anxious to get rid of us?" Sarah asked. "We put you up in our house for a whole week, and this is the thanks we get?"

I said, "I appreciated your hospitality. I really did, but. . . ."

"Sure, you appreciated the price," Bud said. "Here's another word you can use in Scrabble. Maybe you never heard of it — 'hotel.'"

"I would have been happy to stay at a hotel," I said, "but Sarah insisted I stay with you. All my expenses are paid for by the company."

"Yeah, but do they pay for all that gin you drink?" Bud asked.

I said, "I don't normally drink that much, but you kept filling up my glass."

Sarah said, "Oh sure, like Bud was twisting your arm."

Bud said, "There's another word you can use in Scrabble. You may not have heard of it either — 'no.'"

Sarah said, "We would have gone broke if Bud hadn't thought to put cheap gin in the expensive bottles."

"Listen," I said, "I had no idea. I'll send you a check for. . . ."

Mercifully, the public address system interrupted us, calling for me to finally board my flight.

My sister immediately hugged me and began crying, "We don't see you enough, little brother."

Bud put his arm around my shoulder and said, "Anytime you're in town, pal, you stop in and see us. Is that a promise?"

Chick hugged me and shed a few tears, too. "You're my very favorite uncle. I wish you could stay longer."

I boarded the plane and was beginning to load my gear into the overhead bin when I noticed I was missing a small carry-on case. I didn't care. No way was I going back out there.

SPEAK CLEARLY

There's only one reason to go to an airport — to get out of the airport. If you drive there, you want to check your luggage, get on a plane, and get away. If you fly into an airport, you want to rush to baggage claim, get your stuff, and get away. If you are going to pick up someone who is arriving, you want to pick that person up, load up your car, and get away. If you're taking someone to the airport, you want to get that person on board and away. Why? So you can get away.

An airport is a place you go to in order to get away from it.

Airports are confusing places. Baggage comes in and planes go out. There are people getting on aircraft and people getting off. There are corridors that go to Terminal D and corridors that don't go anywhere near Terminal D. There are flight numbers, gate numbers, terminal numbers, and it's all quite indecipherable except to those who must decipher it — the airline and airport employees.

We all turn to them for advice, guidance, and succor. They hold the key to the mystery. They are the only ones who can help us accomplish what we came to the airport to do — to get out of the airport.

They do this by making announcements over a public address system that was probably designed by the same guy who cooks the in-flight meals. I have actually heard people at the ticket counter say, "I think someone just paged me to report to this counter."

The clerk asked, "What is your name, sir?"

He said, "Smith. John Smith."

She said, "We have no message for a John Smith."

Mr. Smith said, "But you just paged me."

She said, "I don't believe we did, sir."

He said, "Then whom did you just page?"

She looked it up and said, "We paged a Mr. Fassad. Ahmal El Faisal Fassad."

He said, "I'm sorry. I must have been mistaken."

She said, "It's quite understandable, sir."

And it is understandable. Over an airport public address system, Ahmal El Faisal Fassad can sound almost exactly like John Smith.

No harm done there, except maybe for Mr. Fassad, who is now upset at someone for not meeting him at the airport. Whoever was supposed to pick him up explained, "But I had you paged."

Mr. Fassad said, "You did not have me paged."

His ride said, "I did."

Mr. Fassad said, "You did not. I listened specifically for a page from you, but all I heard was the airline calling someone named John Smith."

Where there is harm done, though, is when you're waiting to board your flight and you hear the announcement, "Attention all passengers for flight frahm-fram-nine. . . ."

That could have been me. I was on flight 459 and frahm-fram-nine sounds a little bit like that. I decided to pay attention just in case.

The announcement continued. "Flight frahm-fram-nine now ready for boarding at gate flosh-glim D."

I began to panic. I rushed up to a clerk who was waiting on another passenger, and barged in. "Can you tell me if flight 459 is boarding?"

He said, "They'll announce that when it's ready, sir."

I said, "But I think they did announce it."

He looked at me as if to say, "Then why are you asking me?"

I explained. "Well, I'm not sure. They announced flight frahm-fram-nine and I. . . ."

He said, "Sir, we don't have a flight frahm-fram-nine."

I said, "I know, but that's what came over the loudspeaker."

The person who was being waited on said, "Could you please finish issuing my ticket? I was here first."

The clerk agreed with her and said to me, "Just go to your gate and they'll give you more information."

I said, "How do I get to gate flosh-glim D?"

The clerk ignored me, and the customer gave me a dirty look as well as a loud "harrumph."

I heard another announcement reiterating that flight frahm-fram-nine is boarding at gate flosh-glim D. I'd better get there or I'd miss flight frahm-fram-nine, if that was my flight.

I checked the TV monitors and saw that flight 459 was scheduled to depart from gate 41D. Now that could be the English translation of "flosh-glim D," or my flight could have been changed from gate 41D to gate flosh-glim D. Who knew?

I took a chance and rushed to gate 41D just in time to hear the announcement, "Flight frahm-fram-nine is now boarding all passengers from rows frebish to gloffin."

I got in line with my ticket for seat 17B. The attendant returned my ticket and chided me, "We haven't called your row number yet, sir. Please pay attention to the announcements."

I stepped out of line. I thought for sure that 17 came between frebish and gloffin.

Finally, I boarded flight frahm-fram-nine, or 459, which departed from gate flosh-glim D, or 41D, and was seated comfortably in seat 17B, which is about six rows behind gloffin B. I fell asleep.

Then the pilot's voice on the intercom woke me. He said, "To the left of our aircraft, you can see the beautiful Rashnick Clackle of Dashnick."

I went back to sleep. I thought I'd already seen the Rashnick Clackle of Dashnick.

They've got to get better sound systems to make it easier for us to get out of the airport.

ENGLISH SPOKEN HERE . . . AND EVERYWHERE

I don't subscribe to the theory that if you're going to visit a foreign land, you should learn that foreign language. My philosophy is if I'm going to spend my free time sitting on a plane for 12 to 18 hours during my vacation and will be spending my money, then you should learn to speak my language. Comprenez-vous?

Those little phrase books don't help much at all. For instance, I was traveling in a non-English-speaking country once, and I had to converse quickly. I wanted to shout out so that all the locals could understand me, "Stop that man. He has stolen my wallet." I screamed "Hey" and then realized that I didn't know the words for "stop," "man," "stolen," or "wallet." People turned and stared at me wondering why I had shouted out "Hey" for no apparent reason. I quickly reached for my Traveler's Phrase Book.

I felt in my suitcoat pockets, then my trouser pockets, then I wanted to shout out so that all the locals could understand me, "Stop that man. He has stolen my wallet and my Traveler's Phrase Book."

A fellow American tourist came to my aid. She lent me her Traveler's Phrase Book. I quickly leafed through its pages and finally found the word for "Thank you." That shows you how panicked I was. If it had been her phrase book, she probably would have understood "Thank you" in English.

Now I found what I was looking for and shouted out, "Hey . . . I want to buy a bathing cap." What happened was I looked up "thief" in the index and it referred me to 126. I thought that meant page 126, when actually it was directing me to phrase 126.

Of course, by now, the thief was probably in a region that spoke another language. All I could do was turn to the page that told me how to say "Where is the American Consulate?"

My wife, though, does believe in learning a nation's own language. In fact, before our trip to Italy, she insisted that I learn at least the basics of Italian. I memorized "How much do I have to pay?" and "Where is the bathroom?"

I didn't do very well with the first phrase. My spouse and I had a cocktail at the lounge of the hotel where we stayed our first night in Italy. After our drinks, I asked the bartender, or barista as we Italian-speaking people say, "How much do I have to pay?"

The barista said, "Later." So we had another round.

I asked again. He put me off again. We had a third drink.

I asked again; he put me off again. I figured he was having trouble adding up the figures in English.

Then my wife went to the bar and settled the bill immediately. With my faulty pronunciation, instead of asking, "How much do I have to pay?" I was asking, "When do I have to pay?"

I had even more trouble with the second question, "Where is the bathroom?"

While having dinner at one restaurant, I asked my wife, "Where are the men's rooms?" Of course, I asked her in English.

She said, "Ask."

I said, "OK. Where are the men's rooms?"

She said, "I mean ask one of the waiters."

She was trying to turn me into a seasoned, self-sufficient traveler. Instead, she was turning me into a desperate, anxious man who was about to get up and dance the tarantella without music.

She said, "You know the phrase. We studied it before leaving home."

I recited, "Dov'è il cabinetto?"

She corrected me. "Dov'è il gabinetto?"

"Gabinetto," I repeated.

I found a waiter and spoke to him in Italian, "Excuse me."

He turned to me.

I said, "Dov'è il gabinetto?"

He spoke a string of Italian that would take me 12 years to look up in the Traveler's Phrase Book.

I used another phrase I had memorized earlier. "Inglese per favore," which of course means "English please."

He said to me in excellent English, "If you want me to speak in English, why did you ask me in Italian?"

I said, "My wife told me to."

He directed me to the gabinetto. While I was returning to my table, I saw my waiter friend speaking to a group of fellow waiters in Italian. They all tittered as I walked back to my wife.

When I sat down, my wife said, "Come va?" which, loosely translated means, "Did you make out all right?" or "Is everything OK?" or "Did a thief steal your wallet?" or something else. Actually, I didn't care what it meant.

I said to her in no uncertain terms, "Inglese per favore."

She said, "You're no fun."

I said, "There's a group of waiters in this establishment who think I'm hilarious."

She signaled to the waiter. When he came to us, she said, "Il conto per favore." She had been paying all the bills since that episode in the bar.

He said something to her in Italian, and she laughed.

She said something to him in Italian, and he laughed.

He responded, and they both laughed.

I didn't understand a word of it, so I didn't laugh. I did know they were talking about me, though.

When he left to get the bill, I took out my trusty Traveler's Phrase Book and leafed through it, making a few notes on a napkin as I did.

My wife said, "What are you trying to find?"

I said, "Nothing. I'm not going to speak Italian again until I get safely home to my own language."

She asked, "Then what are you looking up?"

I said, "Curses. I may want to mutter a few things under my breath during the rest of the trip."

She then said another word in Italian. I didn't have to look it up.

CHAPTER FOUR

DRIVING

You're allowed to get three questions wrong
on your written test and still get a driver's license.
On the freeway, I sometimes glance over
at the guy driving alongside me at 70 miles an hour
and wonder which three he got wrong.

TRAFFIC IS ALMOST
TWO FOUR-LETTER WORDS

Like most citizens, I spend many hours in the family car. I drive to and from work, to vacation spots, to shopping malls and supermarkets, to visit friends, and to various other destinations. As I drive along, one thought keeps popping into my head — what are these people doing on my roads?

Traffic today is horrendous. It's a result of our nation's good fortune and ready credit. Most families can afford several cars, and those that can't afford several cars have them anyway. Thanks to our economy, America now has a chicken in every pot but so much traffic that we can't get home in time to eat it.

You know what's amazing about today's traffic? All the freeways are loaded with cars and neither the cars nor the freeways are paid for.

When automobiles were first invented, they were a novelty. There was no traffic at all. Then they became more popular and accessible. Traffic would get heavy in one direction during rush hour. Today, traffic is always heavy in both directions. There are just as many people trying to get away from whatever it is you're trying to get to.

We get in our cars, start the engines, drive to the freeways, and sit there. Remember the good old days when the brake was something you used to stop your car? Now it's something you take your foot off of when traffic lets up.

What the instruction booklet I used for my driving test advises for highway driving is ironic: Leave five car lengths between you and the car in front of you. That's fine, but the only way to do that is to talk five people into staying home.

Getting out of traffic is no relief, either, because then you have to try to find a parking place.

When I was a youngster, my dad bought a car — the family's first automobile. It was one of only three or four autos on our block. Dad still took public transportation to and from work. The green Buick was used only for pleasure trips on the weekends. Dad was your typical Sunday driver. Nowadays, though, there are no Sunday drivers. They're all Friday drivers still searching for a parking place.

It's almost to the point now where the only way to get a parking space is to sell the car you're driving and buy one that's already parked.

Of course, I have an assigned parking space where I work, but it's a mixed blessing. It's convenient and it's inconvenient. It's convenient because it's the one the company assigned me and no one else can park in it; it's inconvenient because twice a week, the police tow my car away.

But I'm a survivor. I'm resilient. I'm inventive. I've worked it out so that no matter where I go, I always have an assigned parking space. I've had my name legally changed to "Loading and Unloading Only."

Actually, I got the idea from my wife, who earlier changed her name to "Tow Away Zone."

Years ago, driving was an excursion. Dad would make a big production of it. "Let's go," he'd say, "we're going for a ride."

All of us kids would get excited. Mom, of course, would be harried because this was an unexpected event in her workday. Still, she'd be pleased.

We'd all take our assigned seats in the family car and Dad would lead us on a tour of his "old homestead," the neighborhood where he grew up. Or we'd drive to the airport and watch the planes zoom over our car as they came in for landings. Sometimes we'd drive along the river watching the people sailing or fishing and maybe even stop for a picnic before coming back home. It was relaxed, pleasurable. It was called "Sunday driving."

Driving today is more perilous than pleasurable. It's a white-knuckle ride at breakneck speed. You can't stop and smell the roses because as soon as you slow down, someone honks the horn and gives you a gesture that you've never seen before, don't understand, but whose meaning you are too embarrassed to ask. Driving today is a chore, a responsibility that no one takes too seriously.

I was driving along the freeway the other day, trying desperately to maintain the speed limit while other cars whizzed past me with a sneer. That's right. I don't know how they do it, but rear bumpers of passing cars can actually sneer at a driver who is slowing down traffic by going the legal limit.

One driver was traveling at about my speed, but he kept drifting over into my lane, just slightly, and then he'd pull back into his own. Each time he did, I honked at him — as a warning, you know.

Finally, he slowed so that I could pull alongside him. He lowered his window and shouted, "Can you hold that horn down a little bit? Can't you see I'm talking on the phone here?"

Then he zoomed ahead of me again. Drivers always step on the gas to punctuate their irritation.

I was annoyed, too. So I sped up to get alongside him and started yelling invectives at him. He lowered his window and shouted, "I can't talk now. I'm trying to send a fax to someone" and then put his window up.

Now I accelerated and pulled into the lane ahead of his vehicle. I wasn't being vindictive. I had to get out of the way. I noticed in my rearview mirror that a car was coming at me at a horrendous speed. She wasn't going to slow down, either, because she never noticed me. She was too busy looking into her own rearview mirror and applying her lipstick.

I decided to pull off the freeway and use the surface streets. I put on my turn signal so that I could pull into the exit lane, and the driver graciously let me in. Well, he wasn't that gracious, really; he was just driving a little slower than most of the other traffic. That's because he was reading the morning newspaper at the same time.

Then I had to slow down because of the driver in front of me. He was having his breakfast en route. He was holding a cup of coffee in the hand that was out the window and he was feeding a doughnut or sandwich into his face with the other. He must have been steering with his knees or whatever.

He was going straight, so I turned right, taking an alternate route just to avoid him. At the next red light, I was behind a couple who were more interested in smooching than getting anywhere. When the light changed, they didn't.

I'm in favor of young love, but in a motel or at least on the side of the road. I honked at them. They both gave me a gesture that I'll someday have to ask someone to translate. Then they moved on.

Finally, I passed a car in which the driver was doing nothing but driving. He wasn't reading, eating, snuggling, phoning, faxing — just driving. I got so excited I waved to him as we passed each other at the intersection. Unfortunately, it was an intersection that had a stop sign on one curb and a police car parked at another.

"You know, you went right through that stop sign," the policeman said after taking my license.

"I know, officer, and I'm sorry."

"You've got to keep your mind on your driving when you're on the road."

"Yes, sir."

"I'm going to give you only a warning this time, but I want you to realize that you're a menace to other drivers on the road."

I said, "Well, none of them seemed to mind too much. They were all busy doing something else at the time."

"OK, wise guy, get outta the car."

YOU CAN'T MISS IT

There's a correct and an incorrect way to ask for directions when you're unfamiliar with an area. The correct way is to pull up to a pedestrian who appears to live in the area, roll down your window, and politely say, "Excuse me, but would you know how to get to Main and Market streets from here?"

That person will then get a pensive frown on his face. He'll look in a direction facing Main and Market streets. After a second or two, he'll turn and look in a direction not facing Main and Market streets. Or else, the first direction he looked was not facing Main and Market streets, and the second direction he looked was facing Main and Market streets. You're not sure. He most likely isn't, either.

But he won't admit that.

He'll then give you each and every turn you must take to get where you want to go. Sometimes the turns are indicated by street signs, other times by landmarks. Sometimes both, and occasionally, neither.

Then he ends with, "You can't miss it."

You follow his directions flawlessly and you miss it.

That's the correct way to ask for directions.

The incorrect way is to be visiting a bunch of relatives who live in a town you're not familiar with. Asking any or several of them how to get from here to there is foolhardy. That's how I did it when I had dinner with my nephews, Tom, Dick, and Harry.

"So what are you in town for, Uncle Gene?" Tom asked.

I said, "I have a meeting on Wednesday, but tomorrow I'm going to go visit Aunt Mamie."

Dick said, "Aunt Mamie? Is she still alive?"

I said, "Yeah. She's supposed to be doing pretty well."

Harry asked, "How old is she?"

I said, "I have no idea. But as your grandmom used to say, she must be three days older than God."

Dick asked, "Is she still on the southwest side of town?"

"No," I said, "she moved to a retirement home. I wanted to ask you guys if you could give me directions to get there."

Tom said, "Sure. Where is it?"

I took out the slip of paper I had it written on and said, "It's in Oaktown."

Harry said, "Ohmigosh. That's out in the boonies."

Tom said, "C'mon. It's a half-hour drive."

Harry said, "For people who drive like you, it's a half-hour drive. For people whose wheels touch the ground, it takes an hour and a half."

Tom said, "I'll get you there. What's the address?"

I said, "Anapole and Meager avenues."

Harry said, "Ohmigosh" again. Then he added, "I don't think you can get there from here."

Tom said, "Sure you can. It's right by the Sweet Hills Country Club."

I said, "I don't know where that is."

Dick said, "Nobody does."

Harry said, "You can't get there from here."

I said, "I'd really like to visit Aunt Mamie. She has no family anymore, and she was always so nice to me when I was a kid."

Tom said, "We'll get you there. First you get on the Bell Avenue Interchange. Do you know where that is?"

I said, "No."

Dick said, "Why are you sending him to the Bell Avenue Interchange?"

Tom said, "Because it'll take him right to Hathaway Circle, into the Crosstown Route, then up I-61. Then he'll wind up at Meager Avenue."

Dick said, "But the Bell Avenue Interchange?"

I said, "What's wrong with the Bell Avenue Interchange?"

Tom said, "Nothing."

Dick said, "Everything."

Harry said, "You can't get there from here."

Dick said, "Uncle Gene, you don't want to take the Bell Avenue Interchange."

Tom said, "Why not?"

Dick said, "Because it's not safe. Cars blow up on that road just from nerves."

I said, "I really don't want to get. . . ."

Tom said, "C'mon, they haven't had a major pileup on that road since, oh, last week."

Dick said, "They had a six-car crash this morning. I heard it on the radio."

Tom said, "There you go. It's perfectly safe. They won't have one for another week."

I said, "I'm really not used to driving around here and maybe I should. . . ."

Dick said, "Get on River Road."

Tom said, "River Road?"

I said, "River Road" and wrote it down.

Dick said, "River Road. Now it'll wind around for awhile." Then he asked me, "Are the brakes good on your car?"

I said, "It's a rental. I guess. . . ."

Tom said, "Where's River Road going to take him?"

Dick said, "Across the Franley Bridge and onto I-52. Then he connects to 45 North, comes back down the turnpike, and he's right there."

Tom said, "It'll take him all day to get there."

Dick said, "But he'll still be in one piece. That's better than the way you're sending him."

Harry said, "One problem. I-52 doesn't connect to 45 North."

Harry seemed to be the expert on not getting places.

Dick said, "Sure it does. In Hilltown."

Harry said, "I-52 stops in Avonshire."

Dick said, "It does not."

Harry said, "It does too."

Dick said, "What do you know? You said you can't get there from here."

Harry said, "You can't by going that way. You hit Avonshire, and kaput you're done."

I said, "Look, maybe I can just phone Aunt Mamie and talk to her." Nobody was listening to me.

Tom said, "Bell Avenue Interchange is the best way to go."

Dick said, "You always go these weird ways. I think you have a death wish."

Tom said, "With a brother like you, maybe I do."

I said, "Maybe I'll take a cab." Harry was listening.

Harry said, "Cabs won't go there. They know you can't get there from here."

Dick said, "I'll bet you $5 I can get in my car right now and get over there faster than you can."

Tom said, "Make it $100 and you're on."

Dick said, "Let's go."

I said, "You know something. I never cared much for Aunt Mamie anyway. If she wants to see me, let her come to my hotel." No one heard me.

Tom rushed out and Dick rushed out. This was a fierce competition for pretty hefty stakes now.

Harry sat there with me and said, "My brothers are a little crazy."

I said, "Are they really going to drive over to the retirement home just to see who has the best route?"

Harry said, "Yeah. You know what? One of them could have dropped you off."

I said, "No, they can't get there from here."

Above are the correct and incorrect ways to ask for directions. Neither one works. Get yourself a map.

THINGS THAT GO BUMP ON THE HIGHWAY

I have trouble sewing a button on a shirt. I certainly could never be a tailor, but I can communicate with tailors. I can explain a problem to them so that they understand.

"Sam, I'm not happy with the trousers," I say.

Sam says, "I sewed every stitch personally, with my own hand. I put cuffs on those pants like they were for my own son's wedding."

I say, "Sam, the workmanship is beautiful."

"So what's the problem?"

I tell him. "The right leg is three inches longer than the left."

Sam says, "You don't like 'em like that?"

"No, Sam," I say. "I like both legs the same length."

Sam says, "OK. I'll fix 'em. They'll be ready by Tuesday."

Problem solved. I explain it in layman's terms. Sam understands. The pants will be ready by Thursday, maybe Friday.

Similarly, I have no idea how the post office works. Once I drop a letter in the mailbox, I don't know what processes it goes through. But I can talk to my mailman.

"I think you made a mistake here," I say as I hand him an envelope.

He inspects it and says, "It's addressed to 323 Main Street."

"That's right," I say.

He says, "You live at 323 Main Street."

"I do," I say.

"So what's the problem?" he asks.

I say, "This is addressed to 323 Main Street in Minokosh Falls, Montana, and I live at 323 Main Street in Hockbock, California."

"I see the problem now," he says, taking the letter and driving off.

Again, we have communicated in layman's terms and resolved the issue.

I don't have the same luck with automobile mechanics.

To wit:

A mechanic wipes his greasy hands on a greasier rag and says, "Hi, my name's Earl. What's the problem?"

I say, "The car doesn't have much power and it seems to make a funny noise when I start it up."

"What kind of noise?" he wants to know.

"It's hard to explain," I say.

"Hey, I can't fix it if I don't know what's wrong."

I say, "Here, I'll start it up. You can listen for yourself."

I start the car. It goes vroom-vroom-vroom and then purrs beautifully.

"It's not making it now," I say.

He shrugs. It is his way of repeating, "Hey, I can't fix it if I don't know what's wrong."

"Here, listen," I say. "It goes kind of like 'vroom-vroom-shush-a-shush.'"

He says, "Hey, that's pretty good. Do that again."

I say, "Vroom-vroom-shush-a-shush."

He chuckles. "Hey Charlie, come listen to this."

Charlie, another mechanic, comes over and they both look at me.

So again I say, "Vroom-vroom-shush-a-shush."

Earl says, "This guy does car noises."

Charlie says, "That's really good. Can you do a carburetor with a faulty intake valve?"

I say, "I'm not a professional car-noise impersonator. I'm trying to tell you what's wrong with my car."

Charlie turns to go back to the Buick he has been working on but I hear him whisper to Earl as he leaves, "I hate customers with an attitude."

I say to Earl, "Can you fix it?"

He says, "I don't know. Let's see what we can do."

He goes to one of those immense books that auto mechanics always have on hand and says, "Let's have it again."

I repeat, "Vroom-vroom-shush-a-shush." I am getting pretty good at it by now.

He leafs through the pages of the book. Then he says, "Could you spell that for me?"

"Spell it?" I say.

He says, "I can't look it up in the repair manual if I don't know how to spell it."

"It's a noise," I say. "Shush-a-shush."

"Shush," he says. "Would that be with a 'u' or double 'o'?"

"I have no idea," I say. "It's just a noise my car makes."

Then I get an idea to try a different approach. I say, "It sounds a little bit like when you take a piece of cheese. . . ."

Earl interrupts. "What kind of cheese?"

I say, "I don't know. It doesn't matter."

Earl says, "The more I know about the problem, the better I can fix it."

"OK. Parmesan cheese, all right? It sounds a little bit like when you rub that along a cheese grater."

"Oh," Earl says. He seems to understand that. "What kind of car is it?"

I am pleased we are getting somewhere. I tell him, "A '94 Ford Taurus."

He shakes his head and says, "There's no cheese grater in '94 Fords."

I realize this is hopeless. I fill my car up with gas and take it somewhere else, somewhere where they understand "layman."

A young kid fills my tank and cleans my windshield. I pay him and start the car. The kid knocks on my window. I roll it down and he says to me, "You hear that shush-a-shush noise your car is making when you start it up? You ought to get that fixed. It could cause trouble."

HOW TO TAKE A MOTOR TRIP WITH FRIENDS
— AND KEEP IT FRIENDLY

Long motor trips with friends can become traumatic. Here are some ways to keep the journey friendly:

Hide the Road Map: A driver's worst nightmare can be hearing this from the back seat: "Let me see that map for a minute, will ya?"

I shout, "No."

Despite that, my wife reaches for the map.

I say, "Throw the map out the window."

"He wants to see it," she says.

"Then throw him out the window." I don't want the two of them together.

She hands him the map.

He says, "You know, you're going way out of your way by taking this route. Now, I would suggest. . . ."

I gnash my teeth.

To keep peace among friends on any trip, check the map, plan your route, memorize it, and then eat the map.

Bring Soothing Music:

"Is it OK if I play some tapes I brought along?"

"Sure."

"You like accordion music, don't you?"

"I uh."

"It's my cousin's polka band. Five guys and only one of them has ever had a music lesson."

He puts the tape in. It's terrible.

I ask, "That's not the guy who had the lesson, is it?"

"Nah, he was sick the night they made this tape."

"Pity."

"We don't have to listen to all of it. I just want you to hear the tunes my cousin wrote — just the first 35 songs on the tape."

Bring your own soothing music.

Follow the P-Q-S: Marital discord inside the vehicle should be forbidden.

"I thought you packed my blue sweater, DEAR."

"But you said you were going to pack it. Don't you remember, DARLING?"

Immediately talk with DEAR and DARLING. Explain that they have three choices. They can ride Peacefully, they can ride Quietly, or they can ride Separately — one in the car and one in the trunk.

Play "Fetch & Figure": In a drastic situation, when one of the passengers is more irritating than the rest — to the point of destroying the trip — play this handy automobile game:

Stop at a convenience store and have the offender go in and purchase something — anything. The item isn't important. This is the "Fetch" part of the game.

When this person comes out of the store, he or she has to "Figure" out why the car drove off while he or she was in the store, and abandoned him or her in a strange place. There is no time limit.

HOW TO TAKE A MOTOR TRIP WITH CHILDREN — AND KEEP THEM FROM BECOMING ORPHANS

The opposite of long motor trips with friends is long motor trips with your children. Youngsters tend to become contentious when confined to small areas — like in the same state. In a car they become downright aggressive, like hockey players when exposed to ice.

Youngsters can turn a happy, loving family into the World Wrestling Federation before the trip odometer hits double figures. Their antics can turn brother against brother, sister against sister, brother against dad, sister against mom, sisters and mom against brothers and dad, mom against dad, and any and all other possible combinations.

The only way to combat the unrest is by preparation and careful planning. Here are a few hints that might help:

Pretend to Be Foreigners: This device takes plenty of preparation, but it can be tremendously effective in refereeing family disputes while you are on the road. It works like this:

You begin the journey and travel peacefully for a few miles, and then this happens:

"Daddy, Johnny's hitting me with his elbow."

"I am not, Dad. Sarah's leaning on my side of the seat."

"Am not."

"Am too."

"Am not."

"Am too."

"Johnny just hit me again, Dad. Make him stop."

"I didn't do anything, Dad. Make her stop complaining."

You say, "Je ne comprends pas."

"Mom, can you make him stop?"

"Make her stop, Mom."

Mom says, "No comprendo Inglés."

No matter what complaints the children have, you pretend you don't understand a word they're saying. Eventually, they'll become frustrated with your lack of participation and stop calling on you to settle their disagreements.

They may continue fighting.

"I'm gonna learn to speak French and tell Dad what you're doing."

"Yeah, well I'm gonna learn Spanish and you'll be sorry then."

You don't care what they say. Let them argue and taunt. You and your spouse just drive on peacefully, singing "Frère Jacques" and "La Cucaracha."

Of course, if somewhere during their formative years, you slipped and accidentally spoke to them in English, you've blown your cover. You'll have to try one of these other ploys.

Assign Seats: The airlines do it to maintain decorum. You can, too. In fact, you might even have a podium erected near the door of your house to make the game more believable. Call each child to the counter prior to boarding, write his or her assigned seat on the ticket with a green pen, tell the child that you'll be boarding today by seat numbers, and have him or her wait a little while. If expenses allow, install an audio system in your home so you can call out the children's seat numbers when you're about to depart. If you do it with confidence and panache, the kids may buy it, even enjoy it. It'll make them feel like they're traveling "commercial."

The trick is to plan the seating arrangement carefully. Mix up the sexes. Try not to have boys sitting next to boys . . . or come to think of it, next to girls, either. Conversely, girls should not be next to girls . . . or come to think of it, next to boys, either.

Any two children who are close in age should be separated by a child who is much older or younger. If you don't have the luxury of having much older or younger children, consider delaying the trip until you have a larger, more arrangeable family. Or you might consider borrowing a child for the trip.

Most important, never place any youngster who is prone to car sickness behind your seat. If all of your children are prone to car sickness, don't go.

Sing Happy Songs: Music, to approximate the saying, hath charm to soothe the savage beast. It's a much taller order, but music just might work on your kids, too. Start with songs that are fun and a challenge to sing, something like:

"John Jacob Jingleheimer Schmidt
His name is my name, too.
Whenever we go out, OUT
People always shout, SHOUT
There goes John Jacob Jingleheimer Schmidt
La-la-la-la-la-la-la-la."

Then you repeat it.

"John Jacob Jingleheimer Schmidt
His name is my name, too."

"Dad, Johnny's sticking his tongue out at me."

You shout, in rhythm, "John, stop it."

Johnny says, "Why?"

You say, trying to be reasonable, "You shouldn't stick your tongue out while singing John Jacob Jingleheimer Schmidt. You'll bite your tongue off."

Johnny says, "I'd rather stick my tongue out. I hate this song."

Sarah says, "I hate it, too."

Your spouse says, "I'm not fond of it, either."

You say, "I absolutely detest it."

Sarah says, "Johnny's pinching me."

Johnny says, "Well, she's putting her smelly feet in my face."

You say, "John Jacob Jingleheimer Schmidt
His name is my name, too . . . everybody.
Whenever we go out, OUT
People always shout, SHOUT
There goes John Jacob Jingleheimer Schmidt
La-la-la-la-la-la-la."

Play Some Friendly Family Games: If the singing is more annoying than the bickering, which it tends to be at about the third chorus of any silly song, try distracting the youngsters with some games. There are, actually, some games you can play that aren't associated with a computer.

You say, "OK, Daddy's going to start a little game. Who wants to play?"

Hearing no response, you continue. "OK, I'm going to assign each of you a different color. Won't that be fun?"

Hearing no response, you continue. "Then whenever you see a car of your color, you shout out and say how many cars you've seen. Does everybody understand that?"

Hearing no response, you continue. "Johnny, you'll be blue."

Johnny says, "I want to be red."

"OK, you can be red. And Sarah, what color would you like to be?"

Sarah says, "I want to be red."

"Well, Johnny already has red."

"Why does he have to have red?"

"Because he already has red, that's why. How about if you be yellow?"

"I hate yellow."

"Then you can be blue."

"I hate blue."

"Well, what color do you like?"

"Red."

"You're blue, OK. You're blue."

She's blue.

Sarah asks, "How long do we have to play this dumb game?"

You say, "It's not a dumb game, and we'll play it just until one of you counts up to, oh, let's say one million cars."

Your spouse interjects some reason and fairness and says, "Let's start with 25."

They count up to about four or five cars and then a purple one goes by. They both claim it and start to fight over it.

Sarah says, "Dad, that car was purple but it was blue-purple so it should count as my car."

Johnny says, "It was red-purple so it should be my car."

You say, "Je ne comprends pas."

They both say, "Mom!"

Mom just starts singing, "La cucaracha, la cucaracha."

AIR TRAVEL

*In case of an emergency,
this page may be used as
a flotation device.*

DUMB THINGS I HAVE HEARD
(AND SAID) ON AIRPLANES

"Would you like to check all of your bags through to your final destination?" the airline clerk asks.

"No," the traveler says. "Just the ones I packed and brought with me."

I'm not belittling my fellow passengers, because I'm often as culpable as they are, but there's something about fighting traffic to get to the airport, struggling with baggage, standing in slow-moving lines to catch fast-moving planes, pushing along narrow aisles to get to even narrower seats — something about the entire process that turns our minds into the same stuff with which they foam the runways.

We just blurt out stupid things.

"I fly 100,000 miles a year with this airline." That's my particular favorite. It's usually announced by some businessperson who wants the rest of the passengers to know that he travels extensively. He's an important person in his company — a doer, a shaker, a troubleshooter, a VIP. Maybe he's sent on so many excursions because his co-workers and his superiors can't stand him any more than the particular flight attendant he's now chastising can.

The guy wants special treatment because he flies a lot. Probably way back in 1903 when Wilbur Wright asked Orville to help carry some of the tools back to the bicycle shop, Orville shouted, "I'll have you know I fly 120 feet a year with this airline."

Which brings up an interesting point: What's so special about 100,000 miles? Why is that the cutoff point?

"Excuse me, miss, could you get me a pillow and a blanket, please?" a frequent flyer asks.

The flight attendant says, "I'm sorry, sir, but I think all the pillows and blankets are being used."

"What?" he screams. "I'll have you know I travel 100,000 miles a year with this airline, and I . . ."

"I didn't know that, sir," she says. She turns to another passenger who is sleeping soundly and cozily beneath his blanket.

"Wake up, sir," she says.

He says, "Huh? What?"

She asks, "How many miles do you travel with our airline each year?"

He says, "98,000 miles. Why?"

She says, "Give me the blanket and get your head off that pillow."

She takes them and hands them to the 100,000-mile guy. "Here you are, sir. Sorry about that."

She turns to the other guy and warns him, "Don't try to pull a stunt like that again."

One time, another frequent flyer sat behind me in first class (someone else must have paid for my ticket) and asked the flight attendant, "What time are we due to arrive in Chicago?"

She checked with the flight deck and told him, "We're scheduled to arrive at 5:42 P.M."

He said, "Tell the captain there's a bottle of champagne in it for him if he can get us there by 5:15."

Tell me that this gentleman's brain is not made of runway foam.

Can you imagine what happened when the flight attendant told this to the pilot?

"Sir, a man in seat 3D says that he'll give you a bottle of champagne if you can touch down in Chicago by 5:15."

The pilot said excitedly, "Are you serious?"

"That's what he said, sir."

"Champagne?"

"Champagne, sir."

"That's it, then," he said to his co-pilot. "Give this thing full throttle."

"But we have traffic ahead of us, sir."

"I don't care. Give 'em the horn and pass 'em."

"What if Air Traffic Control objects, sir?"

"Ignore 'em. This is big. We're going for it."

"Whatever you say, sir."

"Oh, and put that seat belt sign on. These passengers are in for a very exciting ride. Man, what I wouldn't do for a bottle of champagne."

Sometimes the brain turns to foam even before you board, especially if there are delays at the terminal.

"I don't know why we have to sit here and wait for the plane to get fixed."

I want to go over to the person who mutters that inanity and say, "I'll tell you why. Because I'm going to be on that plane with you and no way am I going to be taking off in a plane that's broken."

During one very long delay, a passenger went to the ticket counter and asked why we weren't boarding and taking off on our flight to San Francisco.

The clerk explained, "There's heavy fog in the San Francisco area and they're not permitting us to depart just yet."

This man came back later and said, "I just called my brother-in-law who lives in San Francisco. He said he doesn't see any fog there."

This foam-brain didn't realize that there are thousands of flights taking off from airports all over the nation — all over the world. How would he like it if they all called his brother-in-law to check on weather conditions before taking off?

Another impatient passenger asked the clerk, "Why aren't we boarding this plane already?"

The clerk said, "Because there is no plane here yet."

The passenger said, "That's the silliest thing I've ever heard."

No, it isn't. Saying "That's the silliest thing I've ever heard" is the silliest thing you've ever heard.

Here's another one you overhear frequently around airports "I'm not really afraid of flying. I'm just terribly claustrophobic."

Really? I want to ask these people, "What do you do when you drive your car? Do you steer it by running alongside it with your arm clutching the wheel through the open window?"

Another lame expression you sometimes hear on planes is when a husband turns to his wife and says, "As soon as they open that door, I'd like to be the first one off the aircraft."

Good luck. So would 98 percent of the people on the plane with you. And studies show that 74 percent of those 98 percent are going to get off ahead of you.

Here's a dumb statement that needs no elaboration.

The stewardess says, "Which meal would you like, the Chicken Kiev or vegetable lasagna?"

The passenger says, "Which one is better?"

Neither one is.

This one is not frequent, but I actually did hear it.

The flight attendant serving drinks asked, "What would you like?"

The customer replied, "I'd like a Blue Hawaii with extra pineapple juice and hold the umbrella, please."

The flight attendant said, "I'm sorry, we don't serve mixed drinks. We simply have. . . ."

And the irate customer responded, "What are you talking about? Why I'll have you know I fly over 100,000 miles a year with this airline and. . . ."

The brain simply turns to foam.

THE LITTLE TICKET THAT WASN'T THERE

On any trip I've ever taken without my wife, the next to last thing she says to me as I leave the house is, "I love you."

I respond in kind.

The last thing she says to me is, "Have you got your tickets?"

The combination of the two translates to, "I love you, but often you can be a dodo who would forget his head if it weren't attached."

Before departing for one particular trip, I said, "Yes I have my tickets."

She said, "Wait a minute. Normally, when I ask that, you reach into your jacket pocket or inside your briefcase to reassure me that you have your tickets. You didn't do that this time. Why?"

I said, "Because I don't have any tickets."

She said, "You just told me you had your tickets."

I said, "I have my tickets, but I don't have my tickets."

She said, "Are you sure you're well enough to travel?"

I told her, "This is something new the airlines have started. It's called paperless tickets."

She said, "How can you have paperless tickets? That's like having a foodless meal."

I said, "If the airlines could invent that, they'd really have something."

My wife was upset. She said, "All these years, my job has been to make sure that you never went to the airport without your tickets. Now you're telling me that's the only way you can go there."

"That's right, honey," I said. "You've been phased out."

She said, "Replaced by absolutely nothing."

Paperless tickets do take some getting used to. We all like to have something to clutch. If we buy something, we want a receipt. If someone owes us money, we accept an IOU. If we buy insurance, we get a policy. If we hire someone to paint our house, we get a contract. It means nothing, but at least we've got something to hold and read. With a paperless airline ticket, we get nothing. Should there be a dispute, it's our word against theirs.

I mentioned this to the clerk at the check-in counter. I said, "I don't like this paperless ticket thing."

She said, "I'll mention that to management, sir."

That's called the sincerity-less response.

She asked, "Your name, sir?"

I told her. She punched a few keys on her computer and sure enough, I and my tickets were in there.

She said, "You're booked on flight 419 leaving at 2:12 P.M."

I said, "That's correct, but what would happen if that wasn't in there?"

She said, "It would never happen, sir."

I liked her confidence, but I think that's the same thing that Goliath said when someone asked him what he would do if this young kid, David, hit him with a rock.

I said, "But what if it did?"

She said, "It didn't."

I said, "But what if?"

She said, "It won't."

I was going to say, "But what if?" again but decided it was futile.

She said, "You're assigned seat 15A. That's a window seat. Is that what you requested?"

I said, "Yes."

She smiled, but her smile said sarcastically, "How about that? It worked again, didn't it?"

I smiled back at her, but my smile said just as sarcastically, "Someday, Goliath, you're going to sell a ticket to David."

She said, "I'll need a picture ID before I can issue you a boarding pass, sir."

I showed her my driver's license and then said, "What will you do if the Department of Motor Vehicles starts issuing paperless driver's licenses?"

She said, "Then you'd probably be at the DMV counter giving its clerk a hard time and I could move on to the customers who are anxiously waiting in line behind you."

I said, "Do you know why they're anxious? Because they don't trust this new paperless ticket system any more than I do."

She snarled, "Do you have any baggage to check, sir?"

I snapped back, "Yes. I have two pieces."

"Do you want them checked all the way through to your final destination?" she said, still snarling.

I said, "Yes," with a snarl of equal or greater magnitude.

Angrily, she found some baggage tags, tore off the stickers, and went to attach them to my luggage. There was no luggage there.

"Where are your bags, sir?" she asked.

"Right there in front of you," I said, pointing to empty space.

She was confused and looked to me for some sort of explanation.

I said, "That's a new thing I've just started. It's called 'luggageless baggage.'" I was proud of myself and wanted to see how she responded to that.

She simply said, "Security."

I missed flight 419 that day, even though I had a confirmed ticket. Well, I didn't really have a ticket. What I had was a really long hassle with the airline's security forces.

BOARDING BOTTLENECK

Scratch dogs on a certain spot on their bellies and their hind legs will thump with a matching rhythm. It's reflexive. Mention to a school of salmon that it's the first day of mating season and they'll begin swimming upstream like demons. It's instinctive. Broadcast to a group of humans, "This is a preboarding announcement only. In a few minutes, we'll begin regular boarding by row numbers. In order to expedite the boarding procedure, we ask that all passengers remain seated until your seat number is called," and they'll all rush over and crowd around the boarding door.

Why do people do that? Why are they so eager to crowd that boarding gate so they can be among the first to board? It can't be that they're anxious to get to the in-flight food. All passengers, regardless of when they board, will get the same number of honey-roasted peanut packages — one. Could it be that they enjoy getting into that airline seat early so they can sit for a longer time with the seat back in its fully upright, locked, and most uncomfortable position?

A few may say they need the extra time to find their seats. Now that would be reasonable if the seat identification were random. For instance, if seat 7A were located adjacent to seat 26D and right in front of seat 32F, then we all might need extra time to find our assigned seat. But the seats are arranged in numeric and alphabetic order. They're not that difficult to locate.

And there is always a flight attendant on board willing to help. He or she stands at the front of the aircraft right behind the cockpit, looks at your ticket as you board, and then indicates with his or her hand that your seat is located down the center aisle. Which tells you that your seat is either on the right or the left of the aisle and located somewhere behind the pilot's seat. What more help does one need?

Some people rush to the boarding gate as soon as any announcement is made because they don't want to risk missing the plane. Now that's the first logical explanation. I can't tell you how many times that has happened to me.

The clerk at the ticket counter announces that the flight will soon be ready for boarding. Just then, the pilot taxis out to the runway and takes off, leaving all these travelers abandoned in the airport. It's a cruel little joke, but you know how commercial airline pilots are — anything for a laugh.

It has always bewildered me why people must crowd the boarding gate at the first indication that anyone will be allowed on board. I once asked one gentleman why he was standing there.

He said, "Because everyone else is."

I applied some of my mother's homespun logic to that response. I said, "If everyone else were going to jump off the Brooklyn Bridge, would you do it too?"

He said, "No."

I said, "Why not?"

He said, "Because I can't swim."

I said, "You can't get on this plane, either, until your row number is called. Why are you standing here?"

He said, "Because as soon as my row number is called, I can be the first one on."

I said, "Then why don't you stand on the Brooklyn Bridge? As soon as you learn to swim, you can jump in."

He didn't respond to that. He was too distracted and annoyed by a young mother with four children who jostled her way past him and onto the plane. Some people have no consideration.

I said, "You're crowding the boarding area. Why don't you just have a seat?"

He said, "I've already got my luggage over here. If I take a seat, what am I going to do with these 13 pieces of carry-on baggage?"

I said, "Why don't you rent a moving van and drive to Chicago?"

With that, he refused to talk to me any further. He was too busy protecting his carry-on bags and throwing his elbows out to prevent the affluent first class passengers from shoving past him. Elitists.

I think people just feel superior by breaking the rules. That's why folks drive five to 10 miles over the speed limit, roll through stop signs instead of stopping, and stand in front of airplane boarding doors while people traveling with small children or needing a little extra time in boarding are trying to get on.

The airlines should use that to their advantage. Announce, "We're about to open the doors to our aircraft, but our waiting area is quite crowded. Therefore, only people traveling with small children, our first-class passengers, and those belonging to our prestigious 100,000-mile club are permitted to sit in the waiting area."

Everyone will rush to take a seat, and those who are supposed to get on the plane can.

WANDERING LUGGAGE

A man was checking in for his flight to St. Louis. "Do you have any luggage to check?" the clerk asked.

"Yes, I have three pieces," the man said. "I'd like this large one to go to San Francisco. The tan piece I'd like sent to Peoria, and the green suitcase should be delivered to Albuquerque."

The clerk said, "Wait a minute. We can't do that."

The man said, "Why not? You did it last week when I flew to Pittsburgh."

That's a joke.

There are many jokes about how airlines mishandle baggage. Bob Hope has traveled all over the world and even he says, "My ambition is to someday travel to as many places as my luggage has been."

The airlines take a drubbing from the jokesters on this point, and it's really an unjustified attack. I have no idea how many pieces of luggage are handled daily by airlines in airports around the world, but most of it gets safely and securely to the correct destination. It's either waiting for the travelers when they get to the baggage carousel, or it slides down the ramp to be happily reunited with them after a long journey together but in separate parts of the plane.

I've had only one unfortunate incident with misplaced luggage, and it was all Darlene's fault.

I was taking a commuter flight from somewhere to somewhere else about 35 minutes away. This was one of those semi-pro airlines that occupy a shed somewhere near the airport. Its terminal at the airport looks like it was built by the employees. Its ticket counter looks as if it was hammered together by the clerk behind it. Even its planes look suspiciously homemade.

This particular day, Darlene was the ticket clerk, baggage handler, air traffic controller, chief cook, and bottle washer for this company. She may even have been the president, CEO, and owner for all I knew.

She was quite pleasant to deal with — cheerful, friendly, and courteous. I found Darlene, a young blonde with stunning blue eyes, to be quite attractive. She was speaking to one of the pilots when I approached the ticket counter. "May I help you?" she said, looking directly into the eyes of the pilot, who was also young and good-looking.

"Yes," I said and handed her my ticket. She tore something from it, stamped something else, handed me a boarding pass, and said, "I hope you enjoy your flight," all without once taking her eyes off the young, good-looking pilot.

"Is it all right to carry this on the plane?" I asked, showing her my small overnight bag.

"You can do whatever you want," she said directly into the eyes of the pilot. I assumed that was in answer to my question, but I wasn't at all sure.

Later, Darlene led the few of us who were taking this short commuter flight over the tarmac and to the correct plane. Her eyes were focused on the attractive pilot the entire time. Several of us lemmings who followed her could have been sucked into a jet engine and she would never have noticed. Darlene was in love. We were on our own.

At the plane, the pilot stopped me and said, "You can't carry that bag onto the plane."

I suspected that the reason was there's not much room for luggage on these tiny planes. There's room for the passengers only if they hunch over, bend their knees, and walk down the aisle doing an impression of Groucho Marx.

"But Darlene told me I could carry it on," I told the pilot. I turned to Darlene, who continued to gaze lovingly at him. I said, "Miss, didn't you say I could?"

"Thank you for flying with us, and have a lovely flight," Darlene said while fawning over the fly-boy.

The pilot said, "Leave the bag on the tarmac and Darlene will stow it with the other luggage. You can pick it up when we deplane."

I obediently left the bag in Darlene's care and boarded the plane.

We took off with Darlene gazing after the plane that carried her beloved. She watched it taxi, scurry down the runway, and lift into the air. She did all this while still clutching my bag to her breast.

"My bag's not here," I told the clerk at my destination.

He called and spoke to Darlene. Yes, the bag was there at the other terminal. He told Darlene to put it on the next flight and told me that I was welcome to wait for it. It would arrive in about an hour.

I waited and no bag was on the next flight. Apparently, Darlene had fallen in love with that pilot, too.

The clerk was very apologetic, but there would be no more flights that evening. He said, "We'll have it here first thing in the morning."

I said, "No. I'm here just for a dinner meeting. I'm flying back on the first flight out tomorrow morning. Tell Darlene not to ship the bag. I'll pick it up when I arrive there tomorrow." As the clerk was about to call, I asked him to please have that message delivered to Darlene by someone who had no sexual appeal whatsoever.

The next morning, I flew back and approached Darlene. "I'm here to pick up my overnight bag," I said.

She said while gawking at another young pilot, "It'll be waiting for you when you arrive at your destination," she said. "I shipped it out this morning."

I shouted, "This is my destination. I'm not going back to the other airport. I wanted you to hold it here for me."

She said to me, but still looking at the pilot, "You should have had me put a 'Do Not Send' order on it."

I was tempted to shout, "I did," but I didn't want to interrupt young love. Instead, I calmly asked, "Could you call and have them ship that on the next flight? I'll change my flight arrangements and wait for it to arrive."

She did.

I waited.

The bag wasn't on the next flight.

I said, "Why not?"

She explained, "It had a 'Do Not Send' tag on it."

I said, "That was from here. When it was here, you should not have sent it there, but once you sent it there, there was no reason why they shouldn't send it here."

She said, "What?"

There were no pilots in the room. It was the first time I really had Darlene's attention and I blew it with a convoluted sentence like that.

Eventually, I somehow got my bag back and continued my journey to wherever I was going. And eventually, I hope, Darlene will settle down with a good-looking, well-built, prosperous pilot. I hope they have much happiness together and are blessed with rosy-cheeked, gorgeous children. And I hope further that Darlene remembers what she did with them.

THE CARRY-ON-OMANIAC

Have you ever seen those jungle adventure films where the great white hunter, in neatly pressed khaki shorts and pith helmet, trudges through the foliage followed by a procession of natives carrying his impedimenta? Some of them balance the gear on their heads as they march. Others in teams carry poles on their shoulders from which baggage is suspended. Sometimes they chant rhythmical jungle music in some unintelligible foreign language as they march. You're familiar with the image.

That's how I believe this passenger who boarded the flight I was on arrived at the airport. He must have led his baggage bearers through the corridors of the airport terminal straight to the check-in desk. When his row number was called, each of his transporters handed him the bundle he had carried and said, "Have a nice flight, Bwana," or some similar nicety. That's how much carry-on luggage he boarded the plane with.

He hauled all this gear along the narrow aisle of the aircraft, clipping already-seated passengers in the arms and face with the swaying mass of whatever he carried before and behind him. Then he deposited it all on his assigned seat and began the impossible task of finding overhead bin space in which to safely stow his paraphernalia during the flight.

Of course, all of the overhead bins were filled. Planes today are built that way. The last thing they do before a new aircraft is allowed to leave the factory assembly line is to jam luggage into the overhead bins.

Undeterred, this gentleman started with a garment bag that could easily have held all of the costumes for the touring company of the Broadway musical *The Phantom of the Opera*. This bag would hardly fit in my living room, but this traveler was determined to cram it into the diminutive, already occupied, overhead bin. He pushed and shoved and squeezed and pounded. It's difficult to explain how he struggled to pack that oversized bag into an undersized container. The best description is a question: Have you ever seen a teenager eat a hamburger?

In exasperation and some exhaustion, my fellow traveler complained, "Why don't they make something big enough to carry a person's luggage?"

I said, "They do. It's called a moving van."

Well, I didn't actually say it; I thought it . . . loudly. I was going to say it, but then reconsidered . . . for two reasons. First, by nature, I'm non-confrontational — a born coward. Second, he could have killed me and stuffed my lifeless body into his luggage and no one ever would have found me. That, to me, was a distinct possibility. With the amount of baggage he was already lugging around, what's another 160 or 170 pounds of dead weight?

Eventually, he got the bag into the bin, crushing its contents and compacting everything else that was already in that particular overhead bin. Suit coats were squashed, and some poor businessman would be surprised to learn on landing that he had stowed a briefcase and retrieved an accordion.

The bag was in, but the bin door was not closed. And would not close. Could not close. So this gentleman slammed it. He slammed it once. Then twice. Then thrice, fourthce, and fifthce. He slammed it so hard and so often that the captain came on the public address system and announced that we were experiencing a little bit of turbulence.

Our determined bag stuffer did get the door shut. That was one bag down and innumerable more to go. He began the frenetic activity of depositing the rest of his parcels in FAA-approved locations. It was fascinating to watch — sort of like a treasure hunt being run in reverse.

He'd open a bin door and quickly slam it shut again when already-stored valises began to ooze out. When he was successful in finding one cubic inch of available space, he'd wedge in 125 square inches of tote bag. He'd rearrange bags that had been carefully deposited and then rubber mallet his belongings in on top of them. He pushed, he shoved, he punched, he pounded. He got all of his carry-on luggage stored without sacrificing the floor space under the seat in front of him. That was reserved so he could comfortably stretch out his legs, probably the only two bits of carry-on luggage that he should have been permitted.

He settled into the seat next to mine. As we prepared to leave the gate, the flight attendant got on the speaker and said, "Welcome aboard. We'll soon be cleared for takeoff for our flight to Cleveland."

My seat mate said, "What?" He quickly reached into his pocket and pulled out his ticket stub. Checking it, he shouted, "I'm supposed to be going to Chicago!"

He jumped up and began retrieving all of the goodies he had packed into various nooks and crannies of the overheads bins. Hastily, he gathered all of his belongings and raced up the aisle and off the aircraft.

The flight attendant quickly closed the door, the pilot began to taxi out of the gate, and the flight attendant announced, "Now, we can all sit back and enjoy our flight to Chicago."

The ending of that story didn't really happen. But wouldn't it have been nice if it had?

FIRST CLASS, TOURIST, AND PRISONER

I once saw a plaque that read, "A ship is safe in the harbor, but the harbor is not where a ship was meant to be." And a pilot once told me that airplanes are designed to be in the air. In the air, they're graceful and maneuverable; on the ground, they're clumsy and uncomfortable.

Yet many planes are on the ground. They're on the ground for long periods of time. Occasionally, I'm on them. We all have been or will be.

To an airline, you're a potential passenger before you purchase your ticket. After you purchase your ticket, you're a passenger. Once you board the aircraft, you're a prisoner. The captain is your warden. The flight attendants are your guards. You don't even have an exercise yard as the residents of Attica do. You're just on the plane. Your seat back is in its upright and locked position and in a sense so are you.

I boarded a flight in Chicago once, and as we waited on the runway for takeoff, our pilot spoke to us. First of all, I hate pilots speaking to me over the public address system. To me it smacks of arrogance. He's telling us, "I know what's out the left side of our aircraft and you don't."

People in other professions don't announce each move they're making. If your garbage disposal goes, the plumber doesn't announce, "If all those people in or near the kitchen would look under the sink, they could see me now attaching the water input to the side of the new disposal." Kids at the supermarket don't proclaim, "I'm now wheeling your cart full of groceries to your car and will place them in your trunk for your convenience." If people in other professions don't do it, why must pilots?

Nevertheless, our captain spoke to us. "Our takeoff may be delayed for just a few minutes. We have a red warning light in the cockpit." Those are always reassuring words to hear before takeoff — "red" and "warning."

The pilot comforted us, though. "We suspect it's simply a malfunction in the warning light." This didn't comfort me. Whoever made the red light that was malfunctioning might also have made the rest of the plane.

The pilot said, "We'll have it checked, we'll replace the light, and we'll be on our way in about 10 minutes." Have you ever noticed how often this happens? A red warning light in the cockpit malfunctions frequently. Maybe they should go with a different-color light. Red could be the problem. Or perhaps they should start buying their little red lights from some different little red light store.

It wasn't the little red light. This time, it was functioning properly. It signaled that something more serious was wrong. The pilot came on and admitted that. "We're going to taxi to the hangar area and will have some work done on the landing flaps. We should be off the ground in about 20 minutes."

I don't care for unexpected delays when I'm traveling, but I'm always amazed at how impatient fellow travelers can be. And how illogical. Some flyers don't want delays at all.

The captain might announce, "I'm sorry but there will be a slight delay. The left wing of our aircraft just fell off the plane and onto the tarmac. It'll take about 10 minutes to reattach that wing."

Some passengers will say, "C'mon, let's take off. I have a flight to catch in Spokane. I don't have time to wait for a wing to be reattached."

My philosophy, even though I know nothing about aerodynamics, is that if something is wrong with the plane that's going to be hurtling me through the skies at 300 miles an hour about 30,000 feet above the ground, I'd like to have it fixed. And please, fix it while we're sitting still and resting at approximate sea level.

In this instance, the airline personnel agreed with my philosophy. We taxied to some remote part of the terminal, and a truck came out and parked under our left wing. A platform on the truck was raised up to the wing, and workmen began the repairs.

Every 20 minutes or so, the pilot would speak to us again and give us up-to-date noninformation. "The repair crew is still assessing the situation, but its assessment has changed. However, the crew asssures us that when the situation is properly assessed, the repairs will take only about 20 minutes. After that, we can safely begin our takeoff, provided no other red warning lights come on in the meantime."

The only thing we passengers really learned was that after eight of these warnings, which came every 20 minutes, we had been on the ground for more than two and a half hours.

Passengers grew more impatient and hungry. The flight attendants politely told us, "We cannot serve food while we're on the ground." We asked for something to drink. "Against FAA regulations," we were told. How about a cup of coffee? "No," they insisted. If they served coffee now, they'd have none to serve during the flight.

What flight? We couldn't take off with a large repair truck affixed to our left wing, although a few weary travelers among us wanted us to do so. "Tell the captain to take off anyway. I have a flight to catch in Spokane. Those guys on the truck can fix the left wing while we're in flight."

I knew that if they refused to serve coffee, they weren't about to take off with a four-ton truck hanging onto the wing.

More and more of the passengers got restless. A few of the more audacious ones even released their seat backs from the full, upright, and locked positions. Now it was clear we'd never get coffee.

After the seventh hour of this ordeal, people began to get downright rebellious. One man cracked. He kept screaming, "Let me off the plane! I was going to a meeting on the coast. The meeting is now over. There's no reason for me to go. Let me off the plane!"

The flight attendants would not let him off. Why go to all that trouble when the problem would be repaired in 20 minutes?

Insurrection was imminent. Fellow passengers circulated through the plane, furtively whispering, "The breakout is scheduled for 6 P.M. Pass it on."

Finally, a cheer went up from the passengers. Those looking out the left side of the aircraft noticed that the scaffolding was being lowered and the truck was driving away.

We were joyous. We were exuberant. It looked like we might finally begin our journey. Then one passenger destroyed all of our jubilation. He stood up and loudly proclaimed, "Well, it looks like they've finally got the truck repaired."

After an eight-hour delay, we took off, flew safely to the coast, and enjoyed the coffee that the flight crew had cleverly saved for just this occasion. We all enjoyed it except the one guy who had missed his meeting and was not permitted to deplane. He went on a hunger strike.

When we finally reached our destination, we all got off before him. We'd been given time off for good behavior.

Buzzards fly, and so do commercial airlines. Buzzards, of course, flap their wings, but commercial aircraft have fixed wings. Nevertheless, both utilize the same basic principles of aerodynamics to remain aloft. In fact, there are many similarities in the flight of buzzards, and the flight of commercial aircraft. The main difference is that with buzzards the food is usually better.

For one thing, buzzards can dine at a more leisurely pace. They swoop and swerve through the air until they spot something inviting and appetizing. Then they descend and partake. It's relaxed. It's comfortable. And no flight attendants are involved.

On most commercial flights, you are sentenced to dine. Some disembodied, dictatorial voice admonishes you over the public address system, "We are about to begin our meal service in the main cabin and you should remain seated. If you have to go to the bathroom, tough noogies. You should have thought of that while you were in the airport, where there is room to move around, not on an airplane while we're trying to serve your complimentary meal. It's mealtime now, not bathroom time. So just sit still and hold it."

Not only must you remain seated, but you are well advised to remain seated and be vigilant. Know at all times where your legs and elbows are because the cart pushers don't care where your legs and elbows are. They are pushing that cart quickly and efficiently. Their job is to get those hot trays to row 5 immediately. If people happen to be wounded in rows 33, 27, 22, 18, 16, 12, 11, and 7, tough noogies. Remember the flight attendants' motto: "We are here for your comfort and safety, so stay the devil out of our way."

Be a considerate passenger, too, and follow the rules of airline-travel etiquette as laid down by Emily Wiley Post. Don't ask the flight attendants what they're serving. They don't know.

And they don't care.

Oh, occasionally, one or two of them may take the top off and look at the meal, but they still don't know. The dishes are all prepared in such a way that they just look like congealed food. There's no way to tell one from another without sending them off to the FBI lab for detailed analysis.

Don't be fooled by those flight attendants who will answer your question. "This is the beef bourguignonne," or "This is the Chicken Kiev," or "This is the lasagna puttanesca." They're patronizing you. They have no idea what's in those little plastic dishes. All they really know is that it is edible, according to FAA guidelines, and whatever it is, the bottom of it has fused with the little plastic container.

Furthermore, there's really no reason to ask. Every seasoned traveler knows that airlines serve only two meals — chicken and "we're out of that."

If you want something to sip while you're enduring your chicken, tough noogies. That's a whole other cart that hasn't arrived yet. It's still bumping elbows and running over toes of other passengers.

When it does arrive, it's out of whatever you want.

"I'd like a cup of coffee, please."

"Of course you would. I'll be right back with a fresh pot."

You have nothing to wash away the taste of the mystery meal with.

So you just eat your meal. There's nothing else to do. You can't see the movie because the flight attendants are in your way. You can't go to the bathroom because the aisles are jammed with serving carts. So you just eat your meal.

You don't enjoy your meal; you just eat your meal.

Regardless of how many miles you travel, how many countries you visit, how many different airlines you travel on, you will never hear these words on your flight: "Oh, stewardess, could you please get me the recipe for this meal? It was delicious."

Just eat.

If God had meant for us to enjoy flying and dining, He would have made us all buzzards.

FLYING WITH KIDS

Hanging by your thumbs is a bad thing. So is choking on a chicken bone. Getting your earlobe caught under a manhole cover can be unpleasant, too. For sheer annoyance, though, none of these situations compares to flying with a child in your row. The church requires three miracles before a person can be considered for sainthood. In the modern era, though, three trips on an airplane with a toddler next to you or near you is an acceptable substitution.

Flying with a kid other than your own requires saintly tolerance. That's why the FAA doesn't permit parachutes on commercial aircraft, even for the pilot and crew. It's just too much temptation. Rather than sit with an unruly tyke for the duration of the flight, some folks would opt to jump out of the plane, holler "Geronimo," and catch a cab to their destination.

No one under the age of 12 should be permitted to leave the ground. We should pass such a law, and I know the Supreme Court — because those justices fly frequently — would support it.

Why do the airlines permit children to fly? Restaurants have restrictions. "No Shoes, No Shirt, No Service." That makes sense. It keeps the level of the clientele respectable and makes those who do frequent the establishment more comfortable. Airlines might do the same. "No Driver's License, No Voter

Registration, No Seat." Makes sense, but they don't do it. Probably, there are laws against it.

What they could and should do, though, is cancel any flight that has a youngster booked on it. Tell the passengers there's traffic over Chicago or there's fog in San Francisco — any one of those patent excuses that the airlines use regularly. But they don't do that, either.

I think the flight attendants just like to see the passengers suffer. They say to themselves, "Look, all you grownups insist on acting like children when we deal with you, so now you should know what it's like to be around real children."

For whatever reasons, the carriers not only allow toddlers to fly, but they encourage it. The flight attendants give them special care. The pilot even invites them up into the cockpit to see all the fancy buttons and switches, lights and meters. Fine. What we passengers should do is lock the door behind them. Let the pilot endure their tantrums, and crying, and spilling of food and drink. Let us paying customers relax in our uncomfortable seats. They say those big planes fly themselves anyway, so let the pilot baby-sit for awhile and give us some relief. But they don't.

You and I will sometimes have to fly with an under-five seatmate. There are a few rules that may help to make your journey endurable.

Do not acknowledge the youngster. Repeat — do not acknowledge the little ones. Granted they are lovable, and cherubic, but do not acknowledge them. Treat them as you would a discarded wad of gum that's been wrapped in paper and left in the magazine holder in the seat pocket in front of you. Better yet, treat them as you would a discarded wad of gum that has not been wrapped in paper and left in the magazine holder in the seat pocket in front of you. Ignore them. Disdain them. Saying hello to a toddler with a smile and a comforting pat on the head is like feeding a puppy. He will attach himself to you forever. You will become his surrogate parent during the entire trip. He will want to spill his drinks on you, hug you with his sticky fingers, hit you, slap you, scream at you, torment you. All of this while his parents or guardians smile and say, "He doesn't normally take to people this easily. He likes you."

There is no sweeter sound in the universe than the laughter of a child. It's innocent, pure, unadulterated. It resonates with happiness and joy. And each of us adults has some little game our daddy or mommy played with us that we've played with our children and grandchildren. It's a little noise or funny face that is guaranteed to make toddlers laugh. Don't ever play it with a child on an airplane. It may be cute and rewarding to hear that happy child's giggle, but it's neither cute nor rewarding to hear that youngster say, "Again."

And then hear the little one say, "Again," again.

And again, and again, and again.

The game of "Peekaboo, I See You" is adorable the first time you hear chuckles from your little playmate. It becomes painful after 20, 30, or 50 encores.

Games with children are enjoyable when you can walk away from them whenever you chose. They're not enjoyable at 30,000 feet when the seat belt sign is illuminated and the flight attendant won't let you up because he or she is enjoying your in-flight plight.

Some flyers try to pretend they're asleep, hoping this will dissuade children from annoying them. It doesn't. It encourages their mischief. How often do youngsters have a helpless, submissive adult to pick on? Believe me, they will not pass up the opportunity.

Feigning sleep places you at a distinct disadvantage. At least with your eyes open, you can see what's coming. With your eyes closed, you could get hit with a wet lollipop to the forehead; a glass of warm, souring milk to the groin; or a sloppy pacifier stuffed into your nose.

Keep your eyes open and your defenses alert. This is warfare. You're Goliath in battle with David. Take for your own the admonition that referees offer to boxers: "Defend yourself at all times."

Be patient. Be tolerant. Be humane. But when the plane lands, be the first one off. Rush home to your own family. Hug your own grandchildren, but say to them, "Pop-pop's going to go take a nap now."

And do. You've earned it.

ALL RISE

There is a marked difference between the seasoned and the occasional traveler. Take my wife and me, for instance. Being the veteran flyer that I am, I stood up in the aisle of our 737 waiting to deplane (that's what experienced travelers call it). My wife, who travels less frequently, sat patiently in her seat and said to me, "Why are you standing?"

I said, "Because the plane's wheels have touched the ground so everyone on the aircraft must immediately stand up and get their luggage down from the overhead bin. It's the law."

She said, "C'mon."

I said, "Well, it's not an official statute, but it's traditional. People are obliged to stand when the flag passes by, when the national anthem is played or sung, and when the wheels of the aircraft touch the runway."

She smirked. "The flight attendant said that we should wait

until the pilot turns off the seat belt sign."

I told her, "You can't trust flight attendants. She's the same one who told me that they were all out of playing cards when I asked for them. I know they're not all out of playing cards."

My wife said, "But that was the fourth time you asked her. You already had three decks of cards."

"So?" I said. "I don't see any signs posted on this aircraft saying, 'One deck of cards per customer.'"

My wife, who always takes the corporate side of every argument, said, "They don't have to have signs posted. It's common sense — like not standing until the seat belt sign is turned off."

I said, "Honey, look around."

She did . . . with a sneer, which is a step beyond a smirk.

I went on. "Everyone is standing. It's the will of the people."

She asked, "But why are you standing?"

I said, "I don't want to go against the will of the people."

She said, "While we were waiting at the airport, you kept grumbling because you couldn't find a seat. You were annoyed because people had their luggage on the seat beside them."

I said, "So?"

She said, "Well, now you have a seat and you're not using it. Why?"

I said, "So we can get off the plane fast."

She said, "I don't know much about aviation, but don't they have to open the doors of the plane before anyone can get off?"

I said, "Technically speaking, yes."

Now she smirked and sneered, which is a difficult combination to master.

I defended my position. "But when they do open the doors, we all want to get off as quickly as possible."

She asked why.

I said, "So we can all get where we're going quickly."

She said, "We live here. We're not going anywhere. We're home."

I said, "Just because we're not going anywhere doesn't mean we should be late getting there."

She said, "This is foolish. Why don't you please sit down."

I said, "Honey, I couldn't sit down now if I wanted to."

She asked why.

I whispered to her, "Because the guy behind me has his American Tourister jammed into the small of my back."

She said, "Why don't you move forward a bit and then you'll have room to maneuver to sit down like a rational person."

I whispered again, "I can't move forward because the guy in front of me has his briefcase hovering dangerously close to a sensitive part of my body. I saw what he has in that briefcase. It must weigh 73 pounds."

Finally, the doors opened and the humanity jammed into the plane's aisle oozed toward the opening. I blocked the American Tourister guy, who was forcing me forward, so that my wife could escape before me.

My wife stepped off the aircraft. Because I'm the more experienced traveler, I deplaned. I rushed ahead, taking her hand as I went, and pulled her quickly along the jetway.

"What are you doing?" she asked.

"C'mon, honey. Hurry."

She struggled to keep up with me.

I said, "Try and move a little faster, sweetheart."

She gasped, "Why?"

I said, "I want to be the first to the escalator."

We were.

We sped up a tad more and were the first ones at the baggage carousel.

Between breaths she asked, "Why . . . did we run? . . . We still have . . . to . . . wait for our luggage."

I gloated. "But look, we're right by the place where the luggage comes down the chute."

She said, "But it'll take another 10 minutes to get here."

I said, "Yeah, but when it does get here, we'll be the first ones to see it. Isn't travel fun?"

"Not with you," she muttered.

Under my breath, I muttered back, "Amateur."

CHAPTER SIX

HOTELS

This hotel had rooms right on the ocean.
For a little less, it had "ocean-view" rooms, from
where you could see the ocean. I got an economy room,
where the hotel introduces you to a person who knows
what the ocean looks like.

HOTELS ARE FRIENDLY

I like hotels. I really do. I especially like the way they go out of their way to be so friendly. They have someone open the car door for you with a pleasant greeting, welcome you to the establishment, carry your luggage inside, and more. Hotels are friendlier than family.

I visit my brother quite often. I like my brother. I really do. But he never comes out and opens the car door for me. He might help with the luggage occasionally, but he always manages to select the lightest bag. I can't ever recall him putting a piece of chocolate on my pillow before bedtime, and I definitely never get a complimentary round of golf when I stay at his place.

On the other hand, I know of no hotel that ever came out and waffled the school bully for me when he was tormenting me in the third grade. With that one exception, though, hotels have been very magnanimous. I consider hotels my friends. We've grown close over the years.

Because of that intimacy, I feel comfortable speaking my mind frankly to them. This is not in any way a criticism. I relish their friendship and would do nothing to jeopardize it. They know how close our relationship is. Anytime I'm in town, I stay with them, except, of course, when I'm in the town where my brother lives. Then I stay with him. His welcome is not nearly as gracious, but he can beat the hotels prices, barely.

Hotels can improve in some areas, however. Again, I don't mean to find fault. These are merely suggestions that, if implemented, would improve our very healthy relationship and bring us even closer.

The first thing I would recommend is that you hire someone in your — I don't even know what department it would be — probably supplies or furnishings or housekeeping or whatever. I don't know because I'm not that familiar with the inner workings of hotels. I'm always treated so nicely as a guest that I have no reason to know these things. But anyway, in whatever department it is, hire someone who knows the difference between a pillow and a place mat.

Trips tire me out, so I'm always happy to get to my assigned room — the one you've prepared so royally for my arrival — kick off my shoes, lie on the bed, and rest my weary head on practically nothing.

Get some fluff into your headrests. My brother does.

I might also suggest that you have some biology or anatomy lessons for your maids. They do a superb job of keeping the room tidy, the towels fresh and plentiful, and the beds made. But there's the problem. When they make the bed, they should realize that people are going to lie in them, under the covers. When a person lies with his back on the bed and his head resting comfortably on the new pillows I know you're going to get, that person's toes tend to point toward the ceiling. They tend to do that, but only if there's enough slack in the covers to allow those toes to point in that direction.

But the maids pull the sheets too taut and tighten them so rigidly that a person lying down with his head facing north can have his feet go only east and west. No matter how much one tosses and turns during the night, the feet remain facing east and west. It can be painful.

So I ask the maids to loosen up just a bit.

Another recommendation would be to install bathtubs that actually hold water. To me, a bath is soothing and relaxing, especially after a tough day bickering with out-of-town clients. The warm bath is my meditation, my reinitiation into the calm, peaceful world of the spirit.

I love to immerse myself into the warm waters of the bath.

There's no immersion in hotel bathtubs. They don't hold enough water to immerse anything. Lying in a hotel bathtub is like sunbathing on a damp bar rag.

It's not only not relaxing; it's humiliating.

The human body is not always beautiful. At least the one I bring with me on road trips isn't. Under water, it's not bad. But sitting in a small puddle with arms and legs akimbo, it's not aesthetically pleasing.

So get some tubs that hold a reasonable amount of water.

Also, you might think about hiring a mathematician to handle some of your calls. I once made a reservation with a clerk and asked the price of the rooms for that weekend.

"We're having a special right now," he said. He must have recognized me as a good friend. "Those rooms go for $68 a night."

That wasn't bad. I told him that would be fine, but I also mentioned that I had some frequent-flyer coupons that promised me I could get the rooms at half price.

"You're absolutely right," he said. "Let me check. Ah yes, here it is. With the half-price discount, those rooms will be only $66 a night."

I said, "I don't have a pencil and pad with me right now, but I don't think that half of $68 is $66. You might want to check that."

"Well, sir," he said, "the coupons are half off our regular rates. So that does compute to $66 per night."

"I see," I said, not seeing.

So, my good friends in hostelry, maybe you could find a way to make half of $68 a little more than a discount of $2.

And while you're at it, throw a couple extra hangers in the closet. I promise I won't steal them, not from good buddies like you, anyway.

Thanks and keep in touch.

WHERE TO?

There are many rules that travelers should follow. Always have your passport with you if there's a chance you may be journeying abroad. Be sure you have cash or traveler's checks with you. If you're dependent on medicine, make sure you've packed enough to last throughout your trip. And another one I've learned to add to my personal checklist: Make sure you know which hotel you're staying at.

I was in some city, I forget which one, to attend a seminar or give a talk or visit friends, I don't recall, and I went out for dinner. Someone, I don't remember who, suggested a fine restaurant in the area. So I grabbed a cab and tried it.

The restaurant was exquisite, if my memory serves me right, but I was tired from the trip and wanted a good night's rest. I called a cab.

The driver said, "Where to?"

I said, "I have no idea."

He said, "What?"

I said, "I have no idea." I couldn't remember which hotel I

was booked into.

He said, "I don't know how to get there from here."

I said, "I'm staying at a hotel."

He said, "A lot of visitors to our city do that."

I said, "I just checked in and I can't remember which hotel it was."

He said, "Then I guess you're not really staying there, are you?"

I didn't want to keep trading wisecracks with this guy, so I pleaded a bit.

I said, "Look, I'm lost. I checked into a hotel, went out to dinner, and can't remember which hotel it was. Can you help me?"

He said, "Look, buddy. I'm just an ordinary cab driver. I think what you need is the Psychic Hot Line Cab Company."

I said, "Well, I took a cab from the hotel to the restaurant and it took only about 15 minutes to get here. Does that help?"

He said, "Sure. I'll drive for 15 minutes and stop. If there's a hotel there, it'll be yours."

"You're not helping," I said.

"You need a lot more help than I can give, pal," he said.

I said, "Look, I pride myself on being calm, cool-headed, and intelligent. I can logically work any problem out to a solution."

He wasn't impressed. He said, "You should have prided yourself on knowing which hotel you checked yourself into."

I surrendered. I said, "I know this was a very dumb thing to do, but it's not typical of me. There must be some way to find out what hotel I'm at."

He said, "Are you married?"

I was puzzled by the question but answered it anyway. "Yes, I am. Why?"

He said, "Well, your wife probably knows you pretty well. Maybe she sewed the name of your hotel inside your underwear like your mom used to do when you went to camp."

"Very funny," I said.

He agreed and laughed like crazy.

I didn't particularly like this cab driver. I said, "You're a very ignorant man, do you know that?"

He said, "Yes, but I also know where I live."

Then he softened and tried to help me out a bit. He said, "You must have something on you that says where you're staying. How did you know to go to that hotel in the first place?"

I said, "I always carry that information in my briefcase."

"Bingo," he said. "Where's your briefcase?"

"In my hotel room," I said.

"Cancel that last bingo," he said.

Then bits of information started to form in my memory. "It had an awning outside the front door," I said.

He said, "Great. And did it have a guy who opened the door for you and took your luggage inside?"

"Yeah," I said.

"And it probably had a registration desk and all inside."

"Yeah," I said. "Do you know the hotel?"

"Pal," he said, "that's every hotel in this city, in San Francisco, in Des Moines, in Peoria, in Battle Creek. Oh no, wait. There's one in Battle Creek that doesn't have an awning outside."

I could see we were getting nowhere so I said, "Just let me out and I'll find my own way home."

He said, "Wait a minute, pal. The meter's been running all this time. You owe me some money."

I said, "You didn't take me anywhere."

He said, "You didn't know where you wanted to go."

So I got out and paid him his fee. I didn't give him a tip

because I didn't know what to tip somebody who was absolutely no help at all.

I went back in the restaurant, called home, and had my wife tell me what hotel I had mentioned I would be at on this particular day. Then I called another cab.

When I got in, the driver said, "Where to?"

I proudly said, "The Hilton Hotel."

He said, "Which one?"

Always make sure you know which hotel you're staying at.

YOU CAN'T GET THERE FROM HERE

There's a phenomenon that frequently happens in hotels. They host conventions. The AAWM (Association of American Widget Makers) will attract 2,500 members to the same hotel you're staying at. That's acceptable and logical. After all, you can't expect the president of the AAWM to throw an annual convention and hold it at his house. No way. The neighbors would complain about the parking. So they have their gathering at a huge hotel.

You always know when there's a convention at the hotel you've booked. People are wandering around the lobby carrying loose-leaf books with the AAWM logo prominently displayed on the cover. Some folks are wearing various colored ribbons proclaiming them "board member," "regional vice-president," "convention staff," or some other designation. Ninety percent of the people you pass in the hotel are wearing nametags that display their names, hometowns, and company affiliations. That's because AAWM members have notoriously bad memories. They can't recall the names of the people they met at last year's convention. In fact, if the hospitality suites were a success, many of the members don't recall being at last year's convention.

But they're a pleasant, considerate group. They spend most of their day confined to small rooms in the meeting area of the hotel. They'll be locked in with a speaker and some fancy audiovisual equipment learning something that they absolutely must know about making widgets. Some will roam around the corridors or will requisition easy chairs in the lobby to do some important AAWM political lobbying. In the bar at the end of the day, they'll round up a few extra chairs so they can all gather for cocktails around one strategically placed table. They'll be the group in the corner with 65 to 70 chairs gathered around one 14-inch circular cocktail table.

They're ubiquitous but harmless. In fact, most "civilian" patrons of the hotel feel somewhat envious. Those AAWM guys and gals seem to be having a glorious, fun time together. That's great.

The problem is when they have their main event, the annual banquet. This massive shindig is held in the Grand Ballroom, which is usually located on the main floor or the mezzanine of the hotel. That's fine. However, the head honcho of the AAWM is staying in the penthouse suite, which is located on the 28th floor. He or she invites everyone up to have a little cocktail before the big dinner. They all go. You can't be in the widget business and not be seen at this happy hour hosted by the president.

Again, no problem.

They're up there talking, drinking, trading anecdotes, doing some politicking, whatever. It's a pleasant, convivial gathering; no cause for concern for any other guests at the hotel.

The problem develops when someone notices that it's almost time for dinner to be served. Now 2,500 widget makers and widget-maker spouses have to get from floor 28 to the mezzanine. You're a guest on the 12th floor trying to get down to the lobby restaurant for your dinner reservation.

You press the down button to call the elevator, and after a short wait, the bell rings, the elevator doors open, and there are 75 tuxedoed widget makers and spouses crowded into a compartment that should hold a maximum of 20.

They salute you with the drinks they carried from the president's hospitality suite and invite you in. You say, "I'll wait for the next one, thanks."

You push the call button again, the bell tolls, and the doors open to reveal another gaggle of widget makers. Friendly folks. They invite you onto the elevator even though several of them are already being crushed by their fellow widget makers. You decline.

The next four elevators are all packed with widget makers doing their impression of sardines — sardines in formal dress on their way to the gala of the year.

You mentally calculate. Approximately 75 passengers per elevator, multiply by six elevators, divide that into 2,500 widget makers, figure in the time it takes for each car to make the round trip from the penthouse to the mezzanine, and you come to the conclusion that you can't get to the lobby from the 12th floor unless you either are a widget maker or own your own elevator.

So you cancel your reservation in the lobby dining room and instead call room service. They tell you there will be an inordinate delay because most of the staff is busy serving at the Widget Makers' Ball. Those who aren't tied up with that function can't get to your room because most of the elevators are tied up.

So you have a bottle of wine and a few candy bars and snacks from the room's mini-bar. It's not nearly as appetizing nor as nourishing as the fine dinner you had planned to have in the gourmet restaurant, but it costs about the same.

You munch and sip and fume while the widget makers revel in the Grand Ballroom.

OPEN SESAME . . . PLEASE

Men have always been the "openers" of the world. We open the drain when it gets clogged. We open doors for the opposite sex. We open our wallets when the check arrives.

Eve took the first bite of the apple and then invited Adam to snack along with her. However, if those had been stewed apples and stored in a jar, she would have had to get Adam to twist off the lid before she could get to the forbidden fruit.

It has always been thus. Men not only know it and accept it, but we also get a morale boost from knowing there's a chore reserved traditionally for us. Women know it and allow us that satisfaction.

Hotels don't know it yet, at least not the ones that I travel to with my wife.

My spouse and I checked in, and the clerk gave us two little plastic tidbits that looked like credit cards. Those were our keys. We got to our room and set down our luggage in the hallway, and I proceeded to open the door. Well, actually, I proceeded to try to open the door.

I inspected the credit card-like key to make sure I had inserted it correctly. I had done what the instructions imprinted on the card had told me to do but the door didn't unlock.

I tried again. After all, every door deserves a second chance. The lock still wouldn't yield.

"You have to wait for the little green light to go on," my wife advised.

I told her, "The little green light is not going on. The little red light is going on."

She said, "Then you're doing something wrong."

"I'm doing everything right," I insisted. "The little red light is doing something wrong."

My wife suggested, "You have to put it in and pull it out quickly."

I did. The red light went on.

"Now you're doing it too quickly," she told me.

I did it more slowly. The red light went on.

"Now you're doing it too slowly," she said.

"Why don't you try it," I suggested.

She nudged me out of the way and inserted her plastic card. She pulled it out, the green light popped on, and she opened the door. When she reached for her suitcase to enter, I shouted, "Don't go in there!"

She said, "Why not?"

"Because I want to make sure my key works."

"While you're playing with your key, I can be unpacking," she said.

I pulled the door closed.

My wife said, "Now we're locked out again."

"We're not locked out," I said. "I have a key."

"It didn't help you much before," she said.

I put the key in the same way my wife had done, pulled it out the same way my wife had done, and the little red light went on the same way it hadn't gone on when my wife had done it.

I said, "Your key works, but mine doesn't."

She offered me her key. I took it, put it in, pulled it out, and watched the little red light sneer at me again.

I got angry. "Something is either wrong with these keys or with this lock!" I shouted.

She said softly, "Or with you."

"I don't know why they have to use this kind of key anyway," I said.

My wife informed me that it's for security. "It used to be if people found a lost key, they could get into your room and steal your stuff. These keys prevent that."

I said, "If a thief gets into the room, he can't steal my stuff because I can't open the door to get my stuff into the room in the first place."

My wife decided to coach me. "Put it in slowly." I did. "Now pull it out briskly." I did. The little red light went on.

"I just can't learn to use these dumb things," I said.

My wife consoled me. "Oh, c'mon now. You said the same thing about tying your own shoes."

I tried the key again.

And again.

I said, "That does it. I'm going down to the desk to tell them that these keys are not programmed right. When the manager says, 'Is your room satisfactory?' I'll say, 'I have no idea. I haven't seen the inside of it yet.'"

My wife said, "I'll wait here for you."

I stormed off with my plastic key in hand.

Back at the front desk, I was irate. The clerk was condescending. "Are you sure you're using the key correctly?" he asked me.

I said, "Look, I spend a lot of time at hotels. I'm the kind of guy who knows how to get in and out of a hotel room."

He said, "Why don't we just have a little demonstration?"

He brought out a mock-up of the lock mechanism with a plastic key attached to it with a chain. He demonstrated. "You just slip the card in like this, pull it out again, and look." On his mock-up, the little green light went on. This was like kindergarten for key users.

"Why don't you try it?" he said.

I said, "No." It was a no-win situation. If the little red light went on, I'd look like a klutz. If the little green light went on, I'd look like an imbecile. Instead, I said, "Why don't you just reprogram my key."

He did, graciously, but I could see that he was snickering at me on the inside.

He handed me the key and said, "I'm sure this will operate fine now, sir."

"Thank you," I said insincerely.

He asked, "Did your wife's key work all right?"

"No," I lied, and stormed off.

He called after me, "Sir."

I turned. He handed me a couple of pillows.

"What are these?" I asked.

"Your wife called and said there weren't enough pillows in the room. She wanted me to give you these to take back with you."

All the way up in the elevator, I thought to myself, the next time she needs a pickle jar opened, let her call the desk clerk.

WELCOME TO YOU AND YOUR MONEY

Pull up to a hotel — any hotel in any city — and magically, your door will be opened and you'll be greeted with an amiable

"Welcome to our hotel." The trunk will be opened and your luggage toted by a personable bellhop to the check-in desk. You assume that this attention is to make your life easier. You don't have to carry your own heavy bags. Wrong. It's so the hotel can make money. The bellhop with his hand out reminds you that he'd like to make an extra buck or two, also.

The clerk at the desk fawns over you like you're the prodigal son returning to his hotel. He's solicitous, kind, helpful, friendly, courteous, obedient, cheerful, thrifty, brave, clean, and reverent. He's anything you want him to be. He's there to serve you, you believe. Wrong. He's there so the hotel can make money.

Now don't get me wrong. He's genuinely happy to see you. However, he's even happier to see your credit card, which he takes an imprint of to ensure that this hotel makes money.

Another obsequious hotel employee steps up and takes your luggage. This one is different from the one who took your luggage from the car. That one already made his money. This bellhop leads you to an elevator and is concerned about your welfare. "Have you had a pleasant trip so far?" "Are you in town for business or pleasure?" He shows you to your room, shows you how to operate the television and the thermostat, sets your luggage on the luggage rack, and points out any niceties the hotel has to offer. "Have you had dinner? Would you like me to make a reservation?" Does he care if you're hungry or warm enough in the room? Probably a little bit, but he really cares about making some money for the hotel and also a buck or two for his own pockets.

Now you're finally in the room alone. You're free from the obligation to dig out a buck for tipping, to hand over your credit card for an imprint, to enrich your hosts. But are you?

Turn on the television and the first thing you see is a screen telling you that you can watch first-run movies in the comfort of your room. The charge is $7.95 plus tax, and billing is immediate. Is that movie there so you can keep current with Hollywood's latest trends? No. It's there so the hotel can make money.

Of course, there's no obligation to watch the pay-per-view channels that the hotel offers. In fact, you don't even have to watch television at all. You can always take that little key that's attached innocently enough to your room key and open the room's mini-bar. It's loaded with goodies, alcoholic and non-alcoholic. There are candy bars, cookies, cashew nuts, soft drinks, cocktails — all for your pleasure and convenience. Wrong again. It's all there so the hotel can make money. If you doubt that, check the price list: $4.95 for a container that holds maybe eight cashew nuts. That works out to about 61.8 cents per cashew. That works out further to 2.3 cents per cashew for your pleasure and convenience, and 59.5 cents per cashew so the hotel can make money.

Incidentally, the hotel does offer one free service that travelers should take advantage of — the safe at the desk to store your valuables. Use it. Take the key to the mini-bar and lock it in that safe for your entire stay at this hotel.

As with the television, though, you don't have to use the mini-bar. It's simply there (so the hotel says) for your pleasure and convenience. But you're alone in a distant city with not much to do. How do you amuse yourself? Well, you can always talk to your loved ones at home. The room has a phone that is there for your pleasure and convenience. Right? You know the answer by now.

Pick up the phone and the hotel charges you a service fee. It might be anywhere from 50 cents to a buck or two. Place a call and get no answer? Tough. The hotel will probably still charge you the service fee. It's not easy for it to provide these services for your pleasure and convenience. It has to charge you.

Of course, you don't have to use the phone, either. However, just thinking about using it subjects you to a service charge of 25 cents per thought.

So, don't use anything. Just sit there in your comfortable room, which you must admit is neat, tidy, and clean. If you don't believe that, just pick up the little envelope on the desk that has a greeting there from Maybelline, who happens to be your maid who has devoted her services to make certain that your room is neat, tidy, and clean. If you enjoy a neat, tidy, clean room, drop a few bucks into the envelope that is there for your pleasure and convenience, as well as to ensure Maybelline can make a few bucks from your stay at this friendly establishment.

Someone built this hotel not for your pleasure and convenience, but so that it could make some money. Hey, that's fair enough. You've come to this town so that you could do business with someone here so that you could make some money. That's the way of free enterprise.

Just be aware that while you're staying here, free enterprise is not so free.

Nevertheless, there are ways of outsmarting the establishment. I once gave a luncheon talk in a hotel in Reno. Afterwards, I had about a two-hour wait before I had to depart for the airport and my flight home. I decided to have a cocktail to kill some time.

But wait! This hotel had a casino. The casino had slot machines. Play the slot machines and you're entitled to free drinks. Why should I pay for my drinks when I can outsmart the hotel, amuse myself by playing electronic poker for an hour or so, and have the proprietors buy my drinks for me?

So I got a roll of quarters and sat playing poker — as slowly as I could — and waited for the serving girl to take my drink order. I waited and waited and waited.

I played poker and played poker and played poker.

Eventually, she came and took my order, returning much later with my parsimonious cocktail.

That free drink cost me $42.75.

The hotels (and their casinos) are there to make money.

CHAPTER SEVEN

DINING OUT

*Never patronize any restaurant
where "antidote" is listed on the menu
under "side dishes."*

YOUR TABLE IS READY

I'm the kind who doesn't like to take any chances. The sort of guy who wears a belt with suspenders. Anytime we're going out to dinner, I always make a reservation. I just feel safer that way.

"Good afternoon, Phil's Phish Palace. How may I help you?" It was a very pleasant voice on the other end of the line.

"May I make a reservation for this evening?" I asked.

"Certainly, you may," the voice said sweetly. "For what time?"

"8 o'clock, please."

"8 o'clock it is" she said warmly. "And for how many?"

"It'll just be the two of us," I told her.

"And your name?"

"Perret," I said.

"Well, we'll certainly look forward to seeing you and your guest this evening, Mr. Perret."

It was all sweet and light and friendly.

We arrived at Phil's Phish Palace at just about two minutes to 8.

I said to the girl at the reception desk, "Perret. We had a reservation for 8 o'clock."

She said, "I have your reservation right here, Mr. Perret. We're very pleased that you could join us tonight."

I said, "We're looking forward to a pleasant evening and a fine meal."

Everything was so sweet and friendly.

Until she said, "Your table will be ready in about 25 minutes. Would you care to wait in our bar? It's very comfortable."

I said very pleasantly, "If I wanted to spend 25 minutes in your bar, I would have arrived at 7:35, so that after having spent 25 comfortable minutes in your bar, I would then be ready to be seated at my table that was reserved for 8 o'clock."

She said, trying to maintain the pleasantness, "I'm sorry, sir, but I have nothing for you."

I said, "You don't have a table for two?"

She said, abandoning the friendly façade, "I have plenty of tables for two. Unfortunately, they all have two people sitting at them."

I said, "I had a reservation for 8 o'clock."

She said, "I know that, sir, but once people sit down to eat, there's no way we can rush them out."

I insisted, "But I had a reservation."

She said, "I don't know what to tell you."

I said, "Don't tell me anything. Go in there and tell those people that they should get off their rumps and go home."

She said, "It'll be 25 minutes, sir. Should I put your name on the list?"

This is always a tough decision, so I turned to my wife. "It's a 25-minute wait. Do you want to go somewhere else?"

She said, "We don't have a reservation anyplace else."

I said, "Apparently we don't have one here, either."

She said, "Oh, let's just have a drink and wait. It's no big deal."

I said, "Put my name down. We'll be in the bar." I watched to make sure she wrote it down and to note just where on the list we were. I didn't want other people moving ahead of us.

The bar wasn't as comfortable as she said it was, either.

133

"Can I get you folks something?" the bartender asked pleasantly.

My wife said, "Scotch and soda, please."

He said, "You, sir?"

I said, "What do you have for somebody who's in a really rotten mood right now?"

He said, "We have a drink called 'Stingray Saliva.' It's served in a mug shaped like a dead pirate."

I asked, "Is it any good?"

He said, "It's terrible."

I said, "Maybe I should order one and have it sent to the hostess out there."

He said, "Oh, you mean Carla?"

I said, "I don't know her name."

He said, "I do. I'm married to her."

I said, "Oh."

He smiled a particularly sinister smile and asked, "What'll you have?"

I said, "Nothing for me. I'm driving."

He said, "Soon, I hope." Then he left to get my wife's drink.

My wife said, "You make friends everywhere you go, don't you?"

I said, "I'm going out to check on our table."

I asked Carla, "How long a wait is it now?"

She said, "Well, the last time you were here, I told you it would be 25 minutes. So now, I would guess it would be about 23 minutes."

I snuck a glance at her list just to make sure no names after ours were crossed off.

Back in the bar, my wife said, "Why don't you just relax and have a cocktail? It's no big deal."

"I can't have a drink," I said. "Carla's husband might poison me."

"Then just relax," she advised.

I said, "I hate it when you have a reservation and they don't honor it."

She said, "You're being silly now." I hate reasonable spouses. They take all the fun out of being unreasonable.

She said, "You have to wait when you go to the doctor's. That never bothers you. Why is this any different?"

I explained, "Because I like the crab cakes here. I don't like anything the doctor is going to do to me, so I don't mind waiting."

She said, "Well, I'm sure if you asked nicely, Carla's husband would gladly do some things to you that you don't like. Would that make the wait any easier?"

I said, "I'm going to go check on our table."

Carla saw me coming and said, "Just 20 minutes now. Time flies when you're having fun, doesn't it?"

I said, "Are you the one I spoke to on the phone earlier?"

She said, "No, that would be Sarah. She doesn't work nights."

I said, "Oh, I see. You send the nice ones home before the customers arrive, huh."

Back in the bar, my wife was still insisting that I relax. "Have a drink," she said.

"Carla's husband will poison me."

She said, "I know, but with a table for one, I might not have to wait as long."

I went back to check on our reservation.

Carla saw me coming and said, "Well, it's been awhile since you were here last. I was hoping nothing had happened to you."

"Aha," I said. I pointed to the list and told her, "There are names after mine that have been crossed off. How do you explain that?"

She said, "They were pestering me about their reservation so I had them executed."

I sat fidgeting in the bar without a drink while my wife leisurely sipped her scotch and soda.

Finally, Carla came to us and said, "Your table's ready now. I'll take your drinks into the dining room for you."

"I didn't have a drink," I said.

"Wise choice," she said.

After we had been seated at our table for awhile, Carla approached us along with a gentleman in a white jacket and white hat.

She said, "This is our chef, Jacques. I wanted him to meet you, Mr. and Mrs. Perret."

We exchanged pleasantries since I was settled down somewhat by now and eagerly looking forward to Jacques' scrumptious crab cakes.

When the chef left to go back to his cooking duties, I spoke to Carla, pleasantly this time. "Carla, that was very nice of you to bring the chef out to introduce us to him. Thank you."

She said, "I didn't really want to introduce him. I just wanted to point you out to him. Enjoy your meal."

WE SPEAK "WAITER"

When you travel, you eat out a lot. It's a matter of geography. You're, well, wherever you are now, and your kitchen is wherever you were before you went to wherever you are now. And in your kitchen are your cooking and eating utensils — pots and pans, knives and forks, plates, and things like that. Consequently, it's easier to eat out.

Whenever you eat out, you must deal with waiters. Regardless of where you are — Pennsylvania, Albania, Lithuania, or

Transylvania — waiters always speak a foreign language. They speak "waiter."

I first noticed this when I would place my drink orders. I prefer scotch on the rocks and usually order J & B. When the waiter asks, "Can I get you a drink?" I usually say, "I'll have J & B on the rocks with a twist in a bucket, please."

In "waiter," that means something else because when the drink arrives, I taste it and know immediately it's not scotch. I ask the waiter, "What is this drink?"

"It's Jim Beam, sir. Exactly what you ordered."

"No," I said. "I ordered J & B."

In "waiter," that means, "I'm an idiot and don't know what I ordered." So he showed me his order pad and explained, "You ordered Jim Beam, sir. See, I wrote it down."

My wife helped out. She said, "If you say J & B three times real fast, it sounds like Jim Beam."

"But I didn't say it three times real fast. I said it one time in a well-modulated, well-enunciated manner."

The waiter said, "No problem, sir. I'll take your drink back. Now what would you like?"

I said it very precisely. "I would like J & B blended scotch whiskey with ice and a twist of lemon served in a larger-sized glass."

He exited and returned with the wrong drink again.

"What is this?" I asked.

He said, "It's Jim Beam Kentucky straight whiskey served over ice in a regular-sized glass." He showed me his pad, and that was exactly what he had written down.

It was definitely a communication problem.

Many times, a waiter asks, "Are you ready to order?"

I reply, "Give us a few more minutes."

Apparently, though, in "waiter," "Give us a few more minutes" translates to "You may leave the premises now, go out and enjoy yourself, and be back sometime around next Thursday." Because that's what waiters do. They disappear and you can never find them again.

When you do catch a waiter's eye, you ask, "Could you tell us what the specials are?" That's a clear enough request in English, but it has an entirely different meaning in "waiter." In that language, it means "Could you show us all how fast you can talk so that we can't understand one word you're saying?"

When the waiter does this well, which most do, you can't understand anything he said, so you say, "What were they again?"

In "waiter," that means, "That was really neat. Could you do it again even faster?"

When I finally place an order for let's say, filet mignon, the waiter dutifully asks, "How would you like that prepared?"

I say, "Well done, please."

When the dish arrives, I realize that in the waiter's native tongue, "well done" means "Cook the meat so fiercely and so long that investigators can identify which cow it came from only by researching bovine dental records."

As I slice, and chew, and complain, my wife chides me. "You should learn by now. Order your meat medium well."

So the next time I order beef, I tell the waiter, "Medium well, please." When that meal arrives, I discover that the phrase "medium well" in "waiter" means "With a little bit of prayer, tender care, and perhaps some of mother's chicken soup, this piece of meat could easily recover and be well again."

After the meal, a good waiter serves coffee and asks, "Would you care for dessert?"

I say, "No."

In "waiter," that apparently means "Please wheel the pastry cart over to our table and describe in eloquent and hyperbolic terms every calorie- and cholesterol-stuffed item on the tray."

So he does, and I obligingly overindulge.

I pay the check and leave a traditional tip. The waiter says, "Thank you and please come back again soon." That needs no translation. I know it means "I hope I never see you again, jerk."

I'm learning a new language.

HERE'S YOUR ORDER, SIR

One nice thing about dining out is that you have such a rich variety to select from. Most menus offer an abundance of appetizers that are very appetizing. There's a selection of soups and salads. Then, of course, there are the entrées — fish, fowl, meats, and vegetarian alternatives. You can ponder as long as you like and make a choice. You can have whatever you want.

Or can you?

Recently, I went out for lunch. I didn't want much, but I did want something tasty. After studying the menu for a bit, I asked my waiter for half a turkey sandwich with a side of coleslaw. I should have suspected problems as we sparred over the bread.

"Bread?" he asked.

"I'll have that on rye, please."

"White?" he asked.

"No, rye, please."

"Oh, wheat."

"Yeah, wheat'll be fine," I said.

When the meal arrived, it didn't look like my order. First of all, it was a full sandwich; I had ordered half a sandwich.

"What's this?" I asked.

"That's your order," he said.

I said, "No, I ordered half a sandwich."

"Oh," he said, and he checked his order pad. "That's no problem."

But it was a problem because the two halves of the sandwich didn't look like what I had ordered.

I said, "This is tuna."

He said, "Right."

I said, "No, I ordered turkey."

He said, "No, you ordered tuna." He checked his order pad again to make sure he was right.

I knew I had ordered turkey so I shouted to my colleagues at the table, "Did anyone order a tuna sandwich?"

They all stared at me like I was crazy. I took that for a no. So did my waiter.

"That's your sandwich," he said.

I said, "I ordered half a turkey sandwich."

He said, "No, you ordered a tuna sandwich." As evidence, he showed me his order pad. Sure enough, it was right there in pencil — T/CS.

I said, "What does this mean?"

He said, "See? That's a 'T' for 'Tuna.'"

I said, "Turkey begins with a 'T,' too."

He said, "Yeah?" Obviously, he expected me to go on until I made some sort of point.

I said, "What would you have written if I had ordered turkey?"

He said, "But you didn't order turkey."

I asked, "How do you know that?"

He pushed the order pad closer to my nose and said, "Because I wrote down 'T' for 'Tuna.'"

I said, "And to you that proves I didn't order turkey?"

He patiently explained. "Sure. Otherwise I would have written down 'T' for 'Turkey.'"

I impatiently explained, "But don't you understand? 'T' can stand for 'Tuna,' 'Turkey,' 'Tomato,' or 'Tongue Depressors.'"

He said, "We don't serve tongue depressors." He not only missed my order but also my sarcasm.

I said, "May I speak with the manager, please?"

He said, "The manager?"

I said, "The manager."

He left in a huff.

He came back with the chef.

Excitedly, the chef said, "That tuna is perfectly fresh and delicious. I picked it out myself this morning."

I said, "Are you the manager?"

He said, "I'm the chef and I can tell you that this tuna is excellent."

I said to the waiter, "I wanted to see the manager."

He said, "You asked to see the chef."

I said, "Well, whatever I asked for, I'd now like to see the manager."

The chef said, "You're going to tell the manager there's something wrong with my tuna?"

I said, "There's nothing wrong with your tuna sandwich. I wanted turkey."

The chef said, "If you want turkey, you have to ask for turkey. What am I? A mind reader?"

I said to the waiter, "Could you please just bring out the manager?"

The waiter kept pulling the chef back to the kitchen as the chef shouted some foreign, noncooking terms in my direction.

I waited for some time until the waiter returned alone.

"I asked to see the manager," I said.

He told me, "The manager can't come out right now. The

chef has quit."

I said, "What?"

He said, "The chef quit. He said he's had it up to here with people complaining about his tuna."

I said, "I didn't complain about his tuna. I complained about the turkey."

He said, "How can you complain about the turkey? You didn't even order the turkey."

I said, "I did order the turkey."

He shoved that confounded order pad at my face again and taunted me with it. He said in a singsongy voice, "'T' for 'Tuna,' 'T' for 'Tuna,' 'T' for 'Tuna.'"

That was it for me. I was defeated.

I said, "How much for the tuna sandwich?"

He said, "$5.85."

I slammed a five and a one on the table and said, "There. Now I'm going someplace else to eat."

The waiter picked up the two bills and said to me, "I went through all this with you for a lousy 15-cent tip?"

ALL I HAD WAS THE EGG SALAD

I asked a friend of mine how he was enjoying the country club he had just joined. The grounds were beautiful, the clubhouse was elegant, the food was great, the course was kept in fantastic condition, and the golf was superb. He said, "It would be a great club if it weren't for the members."

Travel can be like that, too. It might be a pleasant experience if it weren't for the people. You'd find parking at the airport much easier and faster if everyone else stayed home. The lines going through the metal detectors would be much shorter. Without people on the plane, there'd always be ample room in the overhead bins, the "ocupado" would rarely be "ocupadoed," and there'd be at least a 60-40 chance that they wouldn't run out of the meal you want.

Driving? Well, wouldn't traffic be much more tolerable if you were the only car on the road?

It's people that cause the problems.

When you travel, you're often forced to dine with others. Where you dine and what you dine on is often decided by committee.

"I could go for a nice, juicy steak," Bill says.

"A tender piece of prime rib sounds great about now," Sarah suggests.

"Meat and potatoes sounds good to me," Harry opines.

"I could eat anything so long as it's preceded by a sparkling, dry martini," Charlie volunteers.

So how come we all wind up in some nondescript foreign restaurant eating a gruel-like substance with our hands without a decent drink to wash it down with because they don't serve alcoholic substances for philosophical reasons?

People are the problem, but you can't avoid them on business trips. You travel together, work together, tackle company problems en masse, and eat as a group. It's just the way things are done.

Of course, these joint meals can be fun. Someone in the group can often introduce you to an excellent restaurant that you would never have found on your own. More often than not, the conversation is stimulating and fun. Occasionally, you might even get some company business completed over the meal. And you can have a few laughs and enjoy one another's company — until the check comes.

Then, people again become the problem. More accurately, one person becomes the problem.

That's the person who quickly throws in a $10 bill and says, "All I had was the egg salad."

While the rest of us are stunned, this same person quickly adds, "It was only $8.95. Ten bucks should cover it."

But 10 bucks won't cover it, and he didn't have only the egg salad. He had the egg salad, the tax, and the tip. He also happily partook of the appetizers that we ordered and shared. (He partook, but since he didn't order, he didn't feel he should be charged for the partaking. In his mind, he still "had only the egg salad.") He had several cups of coffee, which restaurants don't give out as bonuses. And he had the pleasure of our company.

Oh, and he also forsook dessert. Oh yes, he forsook it but he also partook of it. He asked the waiter to bring an extra fork, just in case. He doesn't offer to pay for dessert since he didn't order one, but it seems to me that partaking, even partially, of nine other desserts adds up to at least one full dessert. Maybe even a dessert and a half. Nevertheless, his egg salad was $8.95. Ten bucks should cover it.

The rest of us split the bill in even proportions. Someone does the math, adds in a reasonable tip, divides by the number of people there, and comes up with a rounded-out figure of $23 per person. Each person of that "per person" is now subsidizing our friend and his egg salad.

We all pay our fair shares and accept his unfair share.

There are no hard feelings, though. In fact, we even invite our frugal friend to join us for a round or two of nightcaps in the hotel lounge. He suggests that he probably won't partake, but will join us there just to enjoy the camaraderie.

Well, he does meet us in the bar, but we aren't there. While he is waiting for us in the lounge, we manage to get a key to his hotel room, on the pretense of company business. Because he isn't going to drink along with us and share the bill, there is no sense in meeting him in the lounge. Instead, we get all of our cocktails (and a few cans of cashew nuts) from the mini-bar in his hotel room.

Let him explain to the hotel when he checks out that all he had was the "egg salad."

DINNER WITH MY BEST FRIEND

Waldo Winclot is my oldest and dearest friend in the entire world. We have a tradition that goes back a long way, ever since we settled in different parts of the country. Whenever I travel to his hometown, he and his wife take me out to dinner. Whenever he travels to my hometown, my wife and I take him out to dinner.

My wife and I were recently in his city and were driving to meet Waldo and his wife for the traditional dinner.

My wife said while we were driving, "You don't seem to be in a great mood."

I snapped, "I'm in a wonderful mood, and don't you forget it."

"What's wrong?" she asked.

"Nothing's wrong," I said. "I'm fine, wonderful, jolly, happy, delirious. Everything's fine, groovy, terrific, magnificent. Now just leave me alone, will you?"

She said, "Don't you want to have dinner with Waldo and his wife?"

I said, "No, I don't want to have dinner with Waldo and his wife."

She said, "But Waldo is your oldest and dearest friend in

the entire world, isn't he?"

"Yes," I said.

"And hasn't he helped you in your career?"

"Immeasurably," I said.

"You were the best man at his wedding, right?"

"And he was the best man at our wedding," I added.

"You and he talk on the phone three or four times each week, don't you?"

"Yes, we do," I said.

She asked, "Then why don't you want to have dinner with him?"

I said, "Because basically I can't stand the guy."

My wife said, "Maybe I'm missing something, but I don't understand."

"All right," I said, "I'll spell it out for you. We're going to meet them at this restaurant tonight. The maitre'd will greet him and his wife with a big hello and hugs. You and I will be welcomed like royalty. The owner will show us to the best table in the house and buy us a round of cocktails. We'll have a magnificent meal, topped off with after-dinner drinks on the house. And that's why I'm not looking forward to this evening. Understand?"

"Of course," my wife said. "I'd much rather go to a place where they scream at you, make you wait in line, and serve you leftover prison food." I think she was being sarcastic.

I said, "It just bothers me that Waldo's always so superior. His restaurant is always the best, the food is always the greatest. He always knows the owner personally."

My wife defended him. "Waldo's a very outgoing guy. He's friendly, personable, and fun to be with."

I said, "I know. That's why nobody likes him."

She said, "C'mon. Everybody likes him."

"I don't," I said.

She said, "Oh, you like him. Something else is bothering you."

I confessed, "We always have to like his restaurant, his food, his friendly owners and waiters, but when we take him out, he always finds fault. How about the last time he visited us? We took him to a nice place and all he did was complain. He was ticked off because the owner didn't greet us or buy us free drinks."

My wife said, "He was also upset because we had to wait in the bar for two hours until our table was ready."

She was right about that, and I admitted it. "But how about the time before that?" I said. "He and his wife complained about the entire meal. They didn't like the hors d'oeuvres. The veal was too tough. The spinach was sandy."

She said, "No, they were upset because she choked on a piece of glass that was in her potatoes au gratin."

"Yeah, that too, but at the hospital, all he did was moan about the hors d'oeuvres, the veal, the spinach."

My wife said, "You're being very petty about this."

I said, "I've had just about enough of it, that's all. Everything he does is superb. Everything we do is mediocre or downright lousy."

"Well, he does choose lovely restaurants," she said.

I said, "We took him to the finest steak house in town and he didn't like it."

She said, "Oh, c'mon now. What makes you think he didn't like it?"

I said, "Little things. His tone of voice, the expressions on his face, the fact that he picked up his prime rib and threw it against the wall."

She said, "Oh yes, I do remember that."

I had won a small skirmish, so I trudged on. "And we never get to see a menu. His 'finest chef in the world' always prepares a meal especially for us, whether we want it or not. But when we go to our restaurants, he always asks for something that's not on the menu."

She said, "That's just his way."

I agreed. "Yeah, that's his way — to embarrass me every chance he gets."

"You're being too sensitive," she said.

"How about the time he asked if they could make him a plate of angel hair pasta. But he wanted it in a special carbonara sauce, and with little slivers of red and green peppers sliced into it."

She said, "Well, he had a craving for that."

"But we were at a Chinese restaurant."

She said, "They made it for him, though."

I said, "I know, and that makes me hate the guy even more."

The discussion had to end because we came to the parking lot of the magnificent restaurant that Waldo had selected for our evening's dining. Waldo and his wife were waiting at the front door to greet us.

We exchanged warm greetings and friendly hugs all around.

"Waldo," I said, "it's great to see you again."

"Hey, it's good to see you, buddy," he said. "Thanks for coming over."

"Are you kidding?" I said. "We wouldn't miss this for the world."

Waldo said, "You're going to love this place. They've got the greatest chef in the world, and when I told him I was bringing my best buddy in the entire world, he insisted on cooking up a special meal just for us. No menus tonight; the gourmet chef is going to give us his finest. But first, the owner wants to meet you guys. 'Any friend of Waldo's is a friend of mine,' he says. So he insists on buying us a couple rounds of drinks first. How about it? I bet you could use a drink right about now, huh?"

I said, "You bet your sweet. . . ."

"Come along, dear," my wife interrupted.

I went along. I always do. After all, he's my oldest and dearest friend in the entire world.

CHAPTER EIGHT

DESTINATIONS

*I have a book at home that tells me
where I can and can't go on vacation each year.
It's called a checkbook.*

MULE RIDE AT THE GRAND CANYON

I'm never going to ride a pack mule to the bottom of the Grand Canyon. That's not to dissuade others from doing it. I applaud your bravery and, in fact, envy you what must be an exhilarating experience. It's just that I'll never do it.

For one thing, I have a fear of heights. For another, I have a fear of widths — especially on a trip like this. Some of those trails, I've been told by people who've been on this excursion, are only two to three feet wide. That's not nearly enough. Granted, these people may be exaggerating to make their adventure sound more colorful. However, even if they cut the trail in half, that means it's only 4 to 6 feet wide in certain places. Still not enough. Not when one is faced with a freefall of maybe a mile or more.

Reverse the dimensions — a trail a mile or more wide over a drop of say 4 to 6 feet — and I might go along.

I say "might" because I also have a dislike of pack mules, which, in all fairness, is probably mutual. I would never trust my well-being, my life, to a jackass, although with some agents I've had, you might say I've done that with my career.

Pack mules are sure-footed animals who know the terrain and have made the journey hundreds or thousands of times. I know that. Bless them, I hope they make the trip hundreds and thousands of times more — but without me.

And it's more my fault than the mules'. I certainly don't mean to disparage these gentle creatures. Anyone who is the offspring of a female horse and a male donkey has social problems enough without my slander.

It's just that I give off negative vibes. Even if I could work up the courage to sign on for the trip, I know what would happen:

"Howdy. My name is S.S. Calhoun. I'll be your trail boss for the ride."

I shake his calloused hand. "Nice to meet you," I say. "What's the S.S. stand for?"

"Side Saddle," he says. "It has something to do with a rash I had a few years back and the name kind of stuck — along with my underwear for a few weeks there."

S.S. was a Southwest character all right.

He says, "Now for this trip, you're going to need a hat that's tied under your chin, a long-sleeved shirt, long trousers, and sturdy shoes."

"I've got all that," I say.

He says, "Good. Then c'mon over here and say hello to your mule. Pat her on the muzzle and get to know her a little bit."

I do.

"She's beautiful, ain't she?" he says.

I say, "For a mule, yeah. What's her name?"

He says, "Butterhooves."

"Butterhooves?" I say.

He says, "Now every so often along this ride, you, or me, are gonna have to give her one of these pills."

"Pills?"

He says, "Oh, don't worry. It's nothing physical. She's as healthy as a mule."

She is a mule, I think. "Then what are the pills for?"

"Well, they're what you call your antidepressants."

"Antidepressants?"

"Yeah," he says. "She tends to be a mite, uh, suicidal."

I say, "Look, I'm not sure I want to ride around the Grand Canyon on an animal that may decide to end it all — with me astride."

"Now, don't worry about it," S.S. says. "The pills'll take care of that. There's just one little problem."

"Which is?"

"Well, they tend to disorient her."

"Which means?"

"Well, when the other mules turn right to follow the trail, she tends to turn left."

"But there's no trail to the left," I say.

He says, "Well, now, see there. You've captured the problem."

Just then, my wife bounds in and ends my fantasy.

She says, "Sweetheart, the mule ride to the bottom of the canyon was fantastic. The scenery was incredible, the camaraderie unbelievable. I loved it. I wish you had come along."

I say, "Well, I would have, sweetheart. You know how I crave adventure. But I had this chapter to finish."

WATCH OUT FOR THAT METEOR

A few years ago, our family vacationed in Flagstaff, Arizona. Meteor Crater is only about 35 miles east of that city on Interstate 40. So everyone wanted to go sightseeing there.

I didn't want to go. I'm not a crater kind of guy. To me, a crater is just a hole in the ground. It's kind of a pothole with delusions of grandeur.

I imagined this tourist attraction would be an interestingly shaped little cavity that might be paved over and used by skateboarding enthusiasts. It's not. It's a big hole in the ground, 600 feet deep and 4,100 feet across.

The tour guides told us that the crater was formed about 49,500 years ago when a meteor approximately 100 feet in diameter and weighing about 50,000 tons slammed into the Arizona landscape traveling at 43,000 miles per hour. The explosive force of the impact equalled that of more than 20 million tons of TNT and probably extinguished all life within 50 miles of the crash site.

My family toured the crater and the Astronaut Hall of Fame on the grounds, watched the video demonstration, bought a few mementos at the gift shop, and had hot dogs and soft drinks at the cafe. I didn't eat anything. My stomach was feeling a little queasy.

When we got back into the car after our visit, my wife said, "Where should we go now?"

I said, "We're going back to the motel."

She said, "Why are we going back to the motel?"

I said, "Because it has a roof on it."

The kids said, "What are we going to do at the motel?"

I said, "We're going to have our room changed from the second floor to the first floor."

My wife said, "That's silly. Why do we want to move to the first floor?"

I said, "Because the first floor is further away from the sky."

My wife noticed I was pretty jittery as I drove, and figured it out. "You're afraid of meteors."

I told my wife, "I am not afraid of meteors," and then asked my son, "Joey, is your Little League batting hat in the trunk?"

Joey said, "I don't know. Why?"

"Daddy just might want to wear it for awhile if it is."

My wife wouldn't give up. "You are. You're afraid of meteors."

"Well," I said, "this is a meteor-prone neighborhood. It's dangerous."

"There's only one crater," she said.

I said, "It doesn't take many."

"But it happened more than 49,000 years ago."

"That's just it," I said. "If it had happened yesterday, I wouldn't be worried. But 49,000 years ago. We're due."

We drove along for awhile in a silent truce. Then my wife said, "Boy it's hot," and she reached toward the roof.

"Don't open the sunroof," I said.

"It's like an oven in here. Why not?"

"Don't open the sunroof," I said.

My wife said, "Oh no. Don't tell me you're afraid a meteor is going to come in through the sunroof."

"It could happen," I said.

"Do you know the mathematical odds of that happening?"

I said, "I'm not good at math; I'm good at paranoia."

She said, "Closing the sunroof is not going to keep a meteor away."

I said, "Maybe not, but I'd rather be safe than vaporized."

She said, "There's no way a meteor could come through the sunroof."

I said, "Yeah, but what if one does?"

She said, "We'd be destroyed in a flash."

I said, "That's right. And I don't want tourists driving out on Interstate 40 some 59,000 years from now to see the 'Meteor Toyota.'"

Just then, I had to swerve back into my lane to avoid an oncoming truck.

My wife said, "You're driving like a maniac."

I said, "I am not." I swerved out of the way of another truck.

She said, "You're looking up at the sky instead of keeping your eyes on the road."

I said, "Trucks have drivers. They can look out for me. Meteors don't have drivers, so I have to keep my eyes on the sky to make sure one isn't coming."

My wife said, "Pull over. I'm driving."

I pulled over.

My wife took the wheel and cautiously guided us back into traffic on Interstate 40.

She said, "I don't know why you're making such a big deal of this. The man at the crater told us that nowadays it's almost impossible for a meteor to penetrate Earth's dense atmosphere."

I said, "What does he know? He works at a hole in the ground."

And that's the last thing I remember about the trip. Just then, a bug splattered against the windshield, and I passed out.

DELUSIONS OF GUNSLINGING

Tombstone, Arizona, is a great town to visit. It's still thriving in the southeastern part of the state. In fact, it's known as "The Town Too Tough to Die." Unfortunately, that slogan didn't apply to a lot of the residents. In its day, Tombstone was a riotous, rowdy-dowdy, rip-snorting, rootin'-tootin', rough-and-tumble kind of town that attracted some of the greatest gunfighters of the West. Boot Hill, just about a mile north of Tombstone, attracted a lot of the mediocre gunfighters.

A gunfight, of course, was when two citizens had a disagreement that provoked them so much that nothing short of a fight to the death would assuage them. So, the provoker and the provokee would face off in the center of Allen Street, Tombstone's main gunfighting drag. They'd stare each other down with cold, steely eyes. Then with lightning-quick reflexes, they'd unholster their six-shooters and fire.

As the echoes faded into the distant hills and the smoke diffused, the townspeople would say to one of them, "You're the victor." To the other they would say, "Remember, man, that thou art dust and unto dust thou shalt return." And he would — on Boot Hill with the other second-place finishers.

Probably the most famous shootout in history happened at Fourth and Fremont in Tombstone — at the O.K. Corral. In 1881, Ike Clanton and his colleagues engaged in an ongoing, escalating spat with the Earp brothers. The feud finally intensified to the point that Wyatt and his siblings loaded their shotguns and pistols and headed down to the O.K. to give Ike and his associates a little bit of "what for." Doc Holliday wasn't a blood relative of the Earps, but he went, too. Anytime the Earp clan had a fistfight, brawl, group clobbering, or deadly shootout, Holliday was invited. They liked him to share in the family frolics.

At the corral, Clanton probably said something uncivil to the Earp family in general and to Doc Holliday by extension. Wyatt probably said something equally rude to Clanton and his disciples.

Then Ike probably said, "Wyatt, sticks and stones may break my bones, but names'll never hurt . . . Suffering sidewinders! You just shot a hole in my belly."

Then a few more shots were fired and history was written.

That's the way they settled things in Tombstone in the 1880s. There were few lawyers to litigate but scads of gunslingers to agitate and aerate. Gunplay was their favorite form of out-of-court settlement.

The Bird Cage Theatre was a prominent vaudeville house and gambling establishment of that era. It was a tough house to play because the customers were armed and dangerous. If they liked your first show, they'd let you live long enough to do your second show. Tourists can still visit that theatre today in Tombstone and count the bullet holes sprinkled around the walls.

They had itchy trigger fingers in those days. Of course, a lot was itchy back then because they didn't have much indoor plumbing, but they had plenty of outdoor dirt.

Today, Allen and Fremont streets are lined mostly with novelty and gift shops. The O.K. Corral is preserved, but the courthouse where Wyatt Earp and Doc Holliday were tried and acquitted of murder in connection with the O.K. Corral killings is gone. The Bird Cage Theatre, though, is intact, and tourists today can gaze at the house where Virgil Earp and his family lived in Tombstone.

Despite the T-shirt shops and gimmicky saloons and restaurants, a spirit of the gunfighter still pervades the town. I remember when I visited there and walked along the streets where Wyatt Earp wore his lawman's badge, passed the saloon where Morgan Earp was gunned down, and walked by the spot where "Curly Bill" dispatched Marshal White. The spirit of gunfighters past infused my soul.

I began to swagger a bit as I walked.

My wife said, "Did you hurt yourself, dear?"

I said, "No. Why?"

She said, "You're walking funny."

I said, "I'm swaggering."

"Swaggering?" she asked.

"Swaggering," I said. "I'm kind of strutting the way Wyatt Earp must have when his fearlessness and determination brought law to this chaotic mining town. I'm walking with the devil-may-care attitude of Doc Holliday, who didn't fear any gunman's bullets because he knew that he'd already lost the big shootout to the illness that wracked his body."

My wife giggled.

I said, "How dare you laugh, woman." I always call her "woman" whenever I'm swaggering. It helps the image.

She said, "Because you look and sound funny."

I said, "All the big gunfighters swaggered like this."

She said, "Maybe, but all the big gunfighters weren't wearing plaid Bermuda shorts, argyle socks, and blue Hush Puppies when they did it."

She had a point, but it didn't deter me. If I had known the gunfighting legend was going to overwhelm me, I would have dressed the part. I was still going to walk through historic Tombstone with a "don't-mess-with-me" shuffle and with my gun hand poised over my sidearm. Well, it was actually a cell phone hooked on my belt, but I kept my hand on it anyway. It helped my swagger.

I must have captured some of the spirit of those violent men from the past because people noticed me as I walked by. Some stared. A few even backed off when they saw me.

I shouted to my wife, "Have you noticed the attention I'm getting?"

I had to shout at her because she was walking about 10 paces behind me the whole time.

Finally, we decided to take a stagecoach tour around Tombstone. It cost a few bucks, so I paid for two tickets and said, "This is for me and my wife, who's about 10 paces behind me over there." I pointed to her.

She shouted to the attendant, "I'll pay for my own ticket. I never met that man before in my life."

There was only one really comfortable seat on the coach,

and the gentleman who occupied it got up when I boarded and offered it to me. I took it as a sign of respect for anyone who carried himself with the self-assurance that I must have exhibited that day. I was Wyatt Earp. I was Doc Holliday. I was someone who said with his manner, "I'm not looking for trouble, but if trouble comes looking for me, I'll show it the way to Boot Hill."

I settled into the prize seat, and the gentleman who offered it to me leaned over, touched my arm (not my gunslinging arm, thank goodness), and said, "I've seen you walking around town and you seem to be in a lot of pain, so I wanted you to have the comfortable seat."

My wife smirked through the entire ride.

DUDE RANCH

My wife and I visited a dude ranch recently. I don't know why. I either lost a bet or lost my mind, I can't remember which. Don't misunderstand, though, dude ranches are fun and great getaway spots. It's just that I'm not much of a horse and saddle kind of a guy. Even when I was 4 or 5 years old and told my playmates that I wanted to grow up to be a cowboy, they'd say, "Get outta here. You? Get outta here."

I've just never been cut out for cowpunching, even fake cowpunching like they do at dude ranches. One problem is that I don't wear cowboy duds well. Some guys can slip on a pair of jeans, a plaid shirt, a leather vest, and a nifty Stetson and look like Jimmy Stewart. I dress up in the same clothes and I look like Martha Stewart.

I love cowboy hats but can't find one that looks good on me. My favorites are the flat-top ones that Clint Eastwood wore in his string of Western movies. On Clint, this kind of hat looks sexy. When I don a flat-top Western hat, I look like a walking cocktail table.

So I opt for the wide-brimmed style and wind up looking like the Flying Nun. I finally purchased and wore to the dude ranch a 10-gallon Stetson, 9 gallons of which looked just plain dumb.

And I felt awkward in the cowboy boots. I'm not used to wearing high heels. I always felt like I was walking downhill. Even when I was walking uphill, I felt like I was walking downhill. Which confused me. If I fell over, I didn't know which way to roll.

The first thing we did at the dude ranch was get to know the real cowboys who worked there, and they, of course, got to know us. They gave us a test so that they could divide us into groups based on our skills and experience. They'd have us ride and handle some of the equipment. That's what they did with most of the visitors. They took one look at me and just gave me a written exam.

The hardest question was, "Which end of the horse has the ears?" I got it right, but only because it was a multiple-choice question.

Based on performance, the advanced guests were permitted to ride on their own. Other guests would ride the trails only in groups. Me? I was not allowed to leave the room to go to the ice machine unless a wrangler accompanied me.

I persevered. I participated in all the activities — the line dancing, the chuck-wagon meals, the trail rides, the overnight camping where we slept under the stars. I did it all. Not well, but I did it. Then I had a really good day. I only fell off the buckboard twice.

On the last day of the vacation, the dude ranch held a rodeo for the guests, and I was invited to participate.

My wife said, "You're going to do what?"

I said, "I'm in the bull-riding competition."

She said, "You absolutely are not going to be in the bull-riding competition. You call the foreman right now and tell him you're out of it."

I refused. "Sweetheart, they laughed at my cowboy hat. They laughed because I couldn't sit down around the campfire because my jeans were too tight. They laughed when I put on spurs for the first time and tripped over my own feet. They laughed at me at the square dance when I did exactly what the caller said to do and wound up falling into the swimming pool because of it. They laughed at me doing all those things. Did you know that?"

My wife said, "Of course. I laughed, too."

I said, "Well, they're not going to laugh at me because I'm afraid to ride a little old bull."

She said, "Little old bull? Those things weigh more than our Jeep Cherokee."

I said, "So? Once I fall off, the ride is over."

"No, it's not," she said. "That's when the bull tries to gore you, maul you, mangle you."

I said, "So, that's what your friends do when I accompany you to the store for the annual white sale."

She said, "You think this is funny, but it's dangerous. Tell them you quit."

I said, "I can't. They've already assigned me a bull to ride."

"Oh no," she said. "What's his name?"

I said, "Bone Breaker."

She said, "I wonder if it's too late."

I said, "It's too late. I'm not quitting."

She said, "No, I mean I wonder if it's too late to get a double-indemnity clause added to your insurance."

I went to the rodeo and I rode Bone Breaker. Bone Breaker

turned out to be an empty barrel suspended from four ropes that the cowboys jiggled to make the "bull" buck.

In bull riding, you have to stay on for only eight seconds, and they were the longest eight seconds of my life. That's because the ride lasted over 45 seconds. The cowboys and the rest of the crowd were laughing so hard that they didn't want the fun to stop. I was the comedy relief of the rodeo.

I did ride it, though. I cowboyed up and rode that fierce critter. Yes sir, I faced a retired beer container — and won!

Yippee kayoo kayaa!

Next year, though, we're going to a chess tournament.

BOOT-STOMPING KLUTZ

Texas is big. And everything in it is big. That's why the state has to be so big — to hold everything that's in it. You go to a restaurant in any of the other 49 states, order the biggest steak they've got, and they'll broil up a huge slice of beef and bring it to you on a sizzling platter. You order the biggest steak they've got in any Texas eatery and they bring it to you with a cattle prod. Everything is bigger in Texas.

That's where Billy Bob's is. It's the world's largest honky-tonk. But it's more than that. Billy Bob's is its own little world. I really should say its own big world because it's in Texas. It has music, and dancing, and dining and shopping — all in one large, huge, massive, Texas-sized complex. Once you go into Billy Bob's there's no reason to leave. It's like a biosphere for people who like to have fun.

I told my wife that as a treat, "Tonight, we're going to go to Billy Bob's."

She said, "What?"

I said, "We're going to go to Billy Bob's. It'll be fun."

She said, "But you don't like fun. Fun makes you grouchy."

She was right, but I said, "This is my treat for you. This place has one of the world's largest dance floors and we all know how you love to dance."

She said, "I hear they also have 40 bars because we all know how you don't."

She was right again. I'm no Gene Kelly when it comes to dancing. I'm more like Hobo Kelly. I said, "That's my second surprise. I'm going to learn to line dance. Just for you."

She said, "Then let's do it. One way or another, this is going to be a lot of laughs."

First, I had to do some shopping. You know that saying, "When in Rome, do as the Romans do"? Well, you wouldn't have shown up at one of Julius Caesar's parties wearing a leisure suit, and you can't do that at Billy Bob's either.

I went to a local department store and purchased for myself a pair of tight Wrangler jeans, some cowboy boots, a colorful shirt, a fancy belt buckle, and a sexy Stetson. It took 15 minutes to make the purchase and 30 minutes for the sales lady to stop giggling.

When my wife saw me, she said, "Oh my, you look like a different person."

I said, "Sure. Different from when I went in?"

She said, "Different from anything I've ever seen."

I said, "Honey, I have to dress the part. Tonight, I'm going to stomp, slide, bump, and grind."

She said, "I would think that's what you had to do to get into those jeans."

Line dancing is unlike any other kind of dance. It's graceful, rhythmic, and synchronized. It's like that Olympic swimming event only without the water, the slicked-back hair, and those silly nose plugs.

As we entered Billy Bob's, my wife said, "Now you're not going to chicken out on me and just sit there the whole evening, are you?"

I said, "Honey, if I wanted to just sit down, I would have bought the larger-size Wranglers."

No sir, I was ready. These boots were made for dancing, and I wanted to get up there and show off my chops. Besides, Mary Sue, the line-dancing instructor, was a knockout. She was a cross between Dolly Parton and, well, Dolly Parton.

Mary Sue said, "I can make even the clumsiest dancer a pro before this evening is over." She looked at me as she said it.

Mary Sue taught us the moves. Kick, slide, shuffle, slide, kick, slide, turn, shuffle, slide, turn, and repeat.

I said to my wife, "This is easy."

She said, "We haven't started yet."

She was right. We were just reciting the moves, but it was easy.

Then Mary Sue had us walk through those same moves, very slowly. Kick, slide, shuffle, slide, kick, slide, turn, shuffle, slide, turn, and repeat.

It was still easy.

Then Mary Sue said, "Now we're going to add the music. Here we go."

She put a record on, and Hank Williams, Jr. started singing some song about heartbreak and fast living and stuff. Hank Williams, Jr. sings awfully fast.

I began to get confused. I started kicking when I should have been shuffling, and sliding when I should have been turning. There was a very awkward moment when I kicked right, just when the fellow next to me was shuffling left.

Mary Sue turned Hank off, stepped in between me and this other guy, and settled things down a bit.

Mary Sue asked me if I was all right.

I told her I was.

She said. "You just look a little flushed and winded. Why don't you sit down?"

I said, "I'm fine. I'll just stand."

She said, "You know, they make those Wrangler jeans with a roomier waist and bottom."

The others went on with their lesson while I just watched for awhile.

When I thought I had it, I jumped back in the line.

I kicked and I shuffled and I slid but at a different time and in a different direction than everyone else did.

My wife was having a ball, though.

I just kind of slipped out of line. As she was shuffling and sliding, she said to me, "Where are you going?"

I said, "You just keep dancing and having fun. When you're ready to leave, come find me. I'll be at one of those 40 bars."

Just then, some cowboy spun her around. She hollered, "Yee-haw," and had a look of pure delight on her face. She loves dancing.

Mary Sue just had a look of relief on her face.

RAFTING DOWN THE RIVER

Rugged, adventurous, courageous. That's how the brochure described the person who would be interested in a white-water-rafting trip down the Green River in the Utah Dinosaur National Monument. That's when I knew this vacation was for me.

"Rugged, adventurous, courageous?" my wife asked.

"Yes," I said, confidently. "I've been referred to as having those qualities once or twice."

"By whom?" she asked.

"By the person who wrote this brochure," I said.

She said, "He should have been here to care for you when you got the paper cut from opening the brochure."

Her playful little jokes made me even more determined to go rafting. I wanted to prove I was the daring, dauntless thrill seeker that this brochure writer knew me to be. I made reservations and sent a deposit.

I really knew very little about white-water rafting except that I wanted to try it. I said to my spouse, "Honey, what kind of clothes should I bring for an excursion like this?" She said, "Anything that will color coordinate with the yellow streak down your back."

How could she think I'd be scared? I was the one who suggested this vacation. I was the one who requested the brochures. I was the one who made the reservations. I was the one who doubled our life insurance.

She was the one who thought the trip might be dangerous.

I said, "Look, this is a man thing. If you don't want to go, I'll understand."

She said, "I'm going. I was the one who nursed you through the paper cut; I'll see you through this river adventure."

So we went together. All I had to do was promise to paint the outside of the house when the expedition was over.

Our tour guides, who looked like they would have no problem tackling a river or just about anything else for that matter, went over a few basic safety measures with us and then showed us a video of our upcoming journey.

My wife leaned over and said, "This does look a little dangerous."

I chuckled. We rugged, adventurous, courageous people often chuckle in the face of danger.

I said, "Honey, we have experienced guides."

She said, "I guess you're right."

I said, "They wouldn't keep running these trips if they were extremely dangerous."

She said, "I'm just being silly."

I said, "Besides, I'm here to protect you."

She said, "I'm scared again."

But our guides were strong, dedicated, resolute, able to withstand any onslaught. We found that out when we tried to get a refund if we backed out of the trip.

The ride began smoothly. The Green River was enjoyable, pleasant. In fact, it was downright relaxing. It was blue and serene. That's where we were. In the distance, it was vicious, churning, covered with swirling white foam. That's where we soon would be.

We negotiated for a refund and return again. To no avail.

"Don't worry, honey. I'm here to protect you," I said as I slipped my arm around my wife.

We moved into the rapids. The raft bent and twisted and pitched and plunged. The river heaved and sloshed. We were on a roller-coaster ride with no tracks and no safety harness. NO SAFETY HARNESS?

We safely made it through to calmer waters.

I was soaked and exhausted. I turned to my wife and said, "Those rapids were angry, weren't they?"

She glared at me, and I could see that the rapids weren't nearly as angry as she was.

"You let go of me," she said.

"Yes, I did," I confessed.

"You let go of me," she said again.

"Technically, I did. Yes," I confessed again.

"You let go of me," she said yet again.

I said, "Please let go of me." I said that because she had her hands around my throat.

When the rugged tour guide in our raft finally got us separated, I said to my wife, rather hoarsely, "I let go of you for a reason. I thought I was going under and I didn't want to take you with me."

I don't think she bought that logic because it took the rugged tour guide on our boat considerable effort to wrest the oar from her hands so she couldn't swing it at me.

That's the way the rest of the river ride went. It was a memorable adventure. And it wasn't over. I still had the painting to do.

"You know what, honey? I think I'm going to hire someone to paint the outside of the house," I told my wife.

"Really?" she said. "Why?"

I explained, "Well, more people are injured in falls from ladders than from white-water rafting. I think it would be safer to hire a professional."

She said, "I think it would be safer for you to paint the house."

I said, "Really? Why?"

She said, "First because I went on that river ride with you and second because more people are injured by getting waffled over the head with a ladder than from white-water rafting."

I painted the house.

MOUNT RUSHMORE

Mount Rushmore in the Black Hills of South Dakota is a

breathtaking sight. It's not only four of our greatest presidents immortalized in granite, but also the history of our country etched into the side of a mountain. This immense sculpture is a tribute to the spirit, wisdom, and courage that formed, defined, and preserved our nation.

Gazing up at the massive artwork — it can be viewed from as far away as 60 miles — affects you emotionally and spiritually. It gets inside your soul and leaves a message for you there like some sort of ethereal e-mail. Each communication is individualized, different, specific. It communicates something unique to each person who views it.

It certainly left a definite message for me.

In our motel room as we changed for dinner, I confided to my wife. "Honey, I had an epiphany today."

She nodded to acknowledge that she at least heard what I said.

"Guess what it was," I said.

"That you looked up the word 'epiphany' in the dictionary," she said.

"I want to do something great," I told her.

"Terrific," she said. "You can start by repairing the torn screen on the backdoor."

"I don't mean anything trivial like that," I said. "I want to do something that I devote my entire life to. Haven't you ever thought of devoting your entire life to one purpose?"

She said, "Yes. Trying to get you to fix the torn screen on the backdoor."

"I want to have my face carved on Mount Rushmore."

She asked, "Who are you going to replace? Washington, Jefferson, Lincoln, or Roosevelt?"

"I'm not going to replace any of them," I said.

She said, "Well, if you're just planning to squeeze in among them, I have to warn you — it's not easy to nudge granite."

I chided her. "I've made the decision of a lifetime and you're making sport of it."

"I apologize," she graciously apologized. "But how do you plan to go about getting your face carved into Mount Rushmore?"

I told her, "I don't mean Mount Rushmore specifically."

She said, "Maybe you could give the sculptor a head start and pick Mount Baldy."

"Very funny," I said, even though it wasn't. "I would just like to accomplish something so momentous that I would get my face carved into a mountain."

"Any mountain?" she asked.

"Any mountain," I said.

"Even if it's not a famous one?" she asked.

"Well, of course. It'll be famous once I get my face on it," I told her.

She said, "So people will still come here to see Mount Rushmore and then maybe on the way home will stop off and see Mount Whatever?"

"Exactly," I said. "Or, maybe people will stop to see me on Mount Whatever, and then on the way home will stop and take a look at Mount Rushmore."

"You don't think you're getting too cocky about this?" she asked.

"One has to think big if one wants one's face 60 feet high on the side of a cliff."

"So, let me get this straight. The four presidents have to share a mountain, but you're going to get your own summit to smile down from."

"Well, you know me. I'm not a joiner."

My spouse asked, "And what do you plan to do to merit such an honor?"

"I don't know yet," I admitted.

She said, "So you just want to get the carving out of the way first and you'll come up with a reason for it later, when you have more time?"

"No," I told her. "I just haven't thought it all through yet."

She said, "No kidding."

I said, "Did people ask George Washington as a young boy what he was going to do to get on Mount Rushmore? Did they ask Jefferson? Lincoln? Roosevelt?"

She said, "I don't know, but I'm sure if anyone asked those great men to fix the torn screen on the backdoor, one of them would have done it before this."

"You're fixated on that backdoor, aren't you?"

She said, "Well, it's one small step on your journey toward greatness."

"But I want to do something great. Something that will get me up on the side of a mountain."

My wife said, "Well, of course, just fixing the backdoor won't do it. You have to help with the dishes, walk the dog, put your clothes away when you take them off, let me use the remote control once in a while, say romantic things to me every so often. . . ."

I interrupted. "Honey, I don't think you understand. I'm talking about. . . ."

Now she interrupted. She said, "I know what you're talking about. You do those things on a regular basis, and I'll climb up and carve your face into the side of a mountain."

Las Vegas is a friendly town. It's just about the only city in the world that's known by its last name. "Let's go to Vegas," people say. That's friendly. You don't hear other city names so familiarly truncated. Fort Wayne, Indiana, is always Fort Wayne, never "Wayne." It would be sacrilegious to call St. Paul, Minnesota, or St. Louis, Missouri, "Paul" or "Louie." Certainly, no one calls Des Moines by the diminutive "Moines."

But Las Vegas, Nevada, is simply "Vegas" to many because it's a friendly place. There's always a light in the window for weary travelers. In fact, there's a light everywhere in Vegas. The lights flash, blink, strobe, twinkle — do anything to catch your eye. They're calling to travelers, "Come, sit down, have a drink, place a bet, lose a bet, place another bet." Vegas has some astounding theme hotels along the Strip with gaudy, garish facades and ornate, elegant lobbies. The city features the world's finest entertainers. At shows, you can watch Wayne Newton transform a song into an exciting musical experience, or you can watch Siegfried and Roy magically change a leggy showgirl into a sleek, white tiger. Mostly, though, Vegas has gambling.

You can bet on a baseball, football, basketball, or soccer game. You can risk your cash on the roll of the dice, the flip of a card, or the spinning of a wheel. You can gamble while you eat and even while you sleep. Vegas is gambling. It's why it was born and why it can still afford to exist.

My wife and I travel together to Las Vegas from two different points of view. She loves to gamble. She enjoys watching the wheels rotate on the slot machines and listening to the clickety-clank of coins dropping down when the automaton pays off. She loves watching the dealer bust at Twenty-One and donate a few chips to her modest stash. She relishes the excitement and camaraderie around the roulette and craps tables.

I don't.

To me, gambling in Vegas is ordering breakfast from room service at 10:15 when checkout time is noon.

When I was a kid, I bought a double-decker ice-cream cone and stood by the curb outside the store waiting to cross the street. A car went by and some scamp reached out the window and knocked the ice cream from the cone onto the street. I chased that car for three blocks. For 14 cents' worth of ice cream, I chased that car.

In Vegas, I sit down; put $5 in front of me; have a dealer give me a couple of cards, say, "You lose," and take my five bucks. For this, I'm expected to put another chip on the green felt, turn to the person next to me, and say, "Isn't this fun?"

I don't have a gambler's mentality. If I do gamble and I'm winning, the only way to keep my winnings is to walk away from the game. And, of course, if I'm losing, who wants to sit there and keep throwing away cash? So, as soon as I sit down at the table, I want to get up and leave.

But my wife loves it. Why? I don't know. Maybe when she was a kid, no one ever knocked her ice cream off the cone.

Another thing that bothers me about gambling is that my wife is good at it and I'm not. Our first evening in the casino, we each buy maybe $25 worth of chips and then go our separate ways. Within an hour, my chips are gone. I've just had 25 bucks' worth of Rocky Road swatted out of my hand onto the floor. I'm bust.

So I look around for my wife. When I spot her, I casually ask how she's doing. "Not bad," she says. "I had a good run on the slot machines and I'm about 15 bucks ahead."

I'm happy for her, of course. So happy that I want to rub myself down with chicken broth and climb into the cage where Siegfried and Roy keep that white tiger.

Don't get me wrong, Vegas is a fascinating town. Gamblers can go there and have a ball, and so can nongamblers. They just shouldn't go together.

My wife and I have nothing in common once we park the car and check into our room.

"Where do you want to go for dinner?" I ask.

"Gamble," she says.

"Aren't you going to eat?" I ask.

"I can eat at home. When I'm in Vegas, I gamble."

So I eat alone and she gambles alone. She has pretty good luck at the tables; I have bad luck with the meal.

I locate my wife at one of the blackjack tables and since I have nothing better to do, I watch her play for awhile. This bothers her, the dealer, and all of the other players at the table. Finally, she hands me a roll of nickels and says, "Go play the slot machines for awhile." The other players at the table chuckle a tad, probably because they know that the closest nickel slot machines are about 3 1/2 miles down the Strip.

I'm back in an hour. That's 29 minutes to walk there, 29 minutes to walk back, and two minutes to lose the roll of nickels.

I locate my wife at a different blackjack table this time. I watch her gamble for a few minutes and then say, "I'm getting tired. I think we should head up to the room."

She has a 14 showing and asks the dealer for a hit. He turns up a six. She covers her cards with her chips and says, "You go on up. I'll be there in a while."

"When?" I ask.

"In about three days," she says as she collects her winnings from the dealer, who pulled 18.

I go up to bed thinking she's kidding. She isn't. I don't see her again until just before it's time for us to check out.

"Hurry up," she says. "We have to be out of the room before

noon or they'll charge us for another day. I don't know why you have to order room service right before checkout time."

She doesn't understand the gambling spirit that rages within me.

After we check out (I do have to pay for the extra day) and get settled in our car, she says, "I won about $370."

"That's great," I say with the enthusiasm of someone who just had to pay half that amount because his breakfast wasn't delivered until five minutes before checkout time.

My wife says, "We should get away for another long weekend in July. Why don't we come to Vegas?"

I say, "You know, just for a change, I think I'd rather go to 'Moines.'"

She has no idea what I'm talking about, but I don't care.

ELVIS HAS LEFT THE BUILDING, BUT THE ONES WHO THINK THEY LOOK AND SOUND LIKE HIM HAVEN'T

Even for nongamblers, though, Las Vegas is a fabulous sightseeing town. I saw a volcano erupt right on the thoroughfare, in front of the Mirage hotel. I watched pirate ships engage in a fierce battle outside the Treasure Island hotel. I gazed up at the world's highest roller coaster which circles up, down, and around atop the Stratosphere hotel. I saw the light show on Fremont Street. I saw the skyline of New York. I saw the Folies Bergere. I saw Siegfried and Roy (that's a law in Vegas now). And I saw 2,337 people who either looked like or dressed like Elvis Presley.

This is a phenomenon that's unique to Las Vegas. Elvis' talent, and his showmanship certainly earned all the adulation he's received both during and after his lifetime. And he was closely associated with Vegas entertainment. He was a major attraction there for many years and made a movie about the city, and the title song from that film has practically become the town's anthem, "Viva Las Vegas." Nevertheless, if you go visit Hannibal, Missouri, you don't pass legions of people dressed as "Shoeless Joe from Hannibal, Mo." In Waukegan, Illinois, citizens don't dress like Jack Benny and play the violin on street corners. But in Las Vegas, people doll up like Elvis.

After this visit, I formulated three axioms that apply to Las Vegas:

1. Elvis' talent and showmanship have had a profound impact on this city.

2. Anyone, male or female, who can grow sideburns will.

3. A sure way to make a great living is to become a white jumpsuit salesman.

One octogenarian wearing an obvious Elvis wig and sporting a well-worn sequined jumpsuit approached us on the street and began singing "Love Me Tender" to my wife. He wasn't panhandling or being forward. He simply believed that he was "The King" and felt like vocalizing for the lady.

When the song was over, we applauded politely, and I graciously offered him a buck. He refused. He said, "No sir. I don't sing for the money."

I thought that was strange because, after all, Elvis did.

But the old fellow was gracious anyway. Though refusing the tip, he said, "Thangya . . . thangya vermuch."

My wife said, "He was cute."

I said, "OK. If you say so."

She said, "I think he looked a lot like Elvis, too."

I said, "Except that when Elvis opened his mouth to sing 'Love Me Tender,' he probably had more than the one tooth in there."

We took a cab from downtown back to our hotel on the Strip. Guess who our cabdriver looked like? Long sideburns, dark glasses, and a lip that curled up on one side.

"Where to?" he asked with a Memphis accent.

I gave him the name of our hotel.

He said, "Do you know what they call that hotel around these parts?"

I admitted I had no idea.

He said, "They call that place the Heartbreak Hotel." As he pulled away from the curb, he began to croon "Heartbreak Hotel."

My wife and I saw the real Elvis, the original, many times in Las Vegas. On stage, he had energy and charisma, which most of these impersonators can't duplicate. He also had something else that eludes them — he sang on key.

Our cabbie didn't. For awhile, it was hard to decide which annoyed me more, the meter constantly clicking up a higher tab, or this gentleman murdering a very touching song.

Eventually, I decided that the singing irritated me more. I said, "I'll double your tip if you'll stop singing that song."

He said, "I can understand, sir, why you wouldn't want to be reminded of that place. I'll take you to a place with happier memories." With that, he began "Blue Hawaii." It was even more painful.

I said, "Pull over."

He said, in that Memphis drawl again, "We're still four miles from your hotel."

I said, "Close enough."

When I paid him and tipped him, he said, "Thangya . . . thangya vermuch."

We decided to have dinner right there and afterward grab a cab the rest of the way to our hotel. With good luck, we'd catch a cab with a noncelebrity look-alike driver. Or at least one who impersonated Marcel Marceau.

Guess who our waiter was for dinner. Exactly. Another Elvis impersonator with the long sideburns, dark glasses, ornate jumpsuit, curled lip, and accent. He actually sang the menu to us.

I said, "I'll have the 'Love Me Tenderloin,' well done, with the 'Blue Suede Shoes' salad."

My wife had the "You Ain't Nothing But a Hot Dog" with sauerkraut and mustard.

Our waiter said, "Thangya . . . thangya vermuch."

Before our meals came, we were enjoying our drinks. We both ordered something with tiny bubbles in it just to see if a Don Ho look-alike would deliver them. He didn't. I said to my wife, "I think I'm going to take advantage of this Elvis impersonation craze."

She said, "Don't be silly. You don't look anything like Elvis. You're short, overweight, and have thinning hair."

I said, "Exactly. I'm going to dress up like Colonel Tom Parker and manage all the guys who dress up like Elvis."

She gave me a weird look, called over Elvis the Waiter, and ordered a real drink.

FOOTPRINTS IN THE CEMENT OF TIME

What a thrill it was for me to finally stand before the famous Chinese Theatre on Hollywood Boulevard. It was exciting to stroll around and gaze down at the footprints immortalizing so many luminaries of the silver screen, especially for me, who dreamed his entire life of being a rich, famous movie star. The children scampered around, squealing with delight whenever they found a name they recognized — the more recent enshrinees. My wife and I together scouted for those from our era.

I whispered to my wife, "This is inspiring. I feel there's a little bit of all of these movie stars in me."

My wife, who would have preferred a shopping excursion along the renowned and expensive Rodeo Drive in Beverly Hills, said, "I believe that. They seem to have gathered around your waistline."

Her taunt didn't bother me, though. Nothing could bother me now. I was standing before the particular block of concrete that I'd been searching for. I reverently stepped into the footprints.

I said, "Can you believe that John Wayne actually stood on this exact spot?"

She said, "Yes. I would imagine that's how his footprints got there."

I hardly heard what my wife was saying. I was lost in reverie.

"John Wayne," I said respectfully. "The only man who conquered the Wild West and won World War II all in the same lifetime."

My wife said nothing, so I tried to impress her with how august this simple concrete shrine was to me.

I said, "As a young child, I always dreamed of becoming a Western star."

"Why didn't you?" she asked.

"I never learned to ride a horse," I said.

She said, "You could have been a Western hero who took a cab everywhere he went."

I said, "Don't make sport of me. It was my goal, my ambition, my destination. I would have done anything to achieve it."

"Then why didn't you learn to ride a horse?"

"We lived in a small row house in the city. I shared a bedroom with two older brothers."

She said, "So?"

I said, "Well, they didn't want to share their bedroom with my faithful horse, Thunder."

"Thunder?" she repeated.

"Thunder," I said. "So named because he could run as fast as lightning."

"Why didn't you name him Lightning, then?" she asked.

"Because Lightning was already taken," I explained. "Jimmy down the street also wanted to be a cowboy star and he'd already named his imaginary horse Lightning."

She said, "So you never had a real horse."

I said, "No, but I did have a real guitar."

"You still do," she said.

I said, "Yes, but I don't play it much anymore."

She said, "And I appreciate that."

I told her, "I always wanted to be a Western movie star and have a funny old-timer with a scraggly grey beard as my sidekick."

"And what was I? Your second choice?"

"I wanted to be a singing cowboy."

She said, "That would have made Geronimo surrender sooner."

I said, "I dreamed of riding my horse across the wide-open prairie, singing my Western songs and strumming my guitar."

She said, "I don't think so. You play the guitar badly enough when you're just sitting still."

"And this man, whose footprints I'm standing in, was my idol, my inspiration, my mentor. Let me show you my John Wayne walk." I backed up a few steps and then walked toward my spouse with my version of John Wayne's frontier swagger.

I said, "What do you think? Doesn't that walk remind you of The Duke?"

She said, "Maybe Patty Duke."

"I even trained myself to talk like him," I said. "Listen to this." I did my impression of John Wayne's strong yet dulcet tones. "Listen, Pilgrim, this town's not big enough for the two of us."

I waited for approbation. None came.

I asked, "Well, what did you think of my impression?"

She said, "It makes your guitar playing sound good."

It didn't matter. I didn't need her approval. This moment was between me and John Wayne's footprints. I stepped into them again, and as my tribute to The Duke and his work, I sang the entire first verse of "Red River Valley."

Other tourists stared at me in open-mouthed wonder. A few backed away — in awe, I suppose.

My wife grabbed and shook my arm and said, "C'mon, you've seen the footprints, now let's go to Rodeo Drive."

I said, "I'd much rather linger here."

She said, "I want to do some shopping. Maybe I'll buy you a cowboy suit."

"All right," I said. "We'll go shopping." But I had one last salute to the great John Wayne left in me. Instead of just calling to the kids, I motioned them forward with the same motion and yell that The Duke used as the trail boss in "Red River Valley." I swung my arm forward, yelled "Hiiiii Yooooo," and marched along the pavement with my John Wayne strut.

It must have been very impressive, too, because as I walked away, many of the other tourists began applauding my exit.

Cow Pie Ain't No Dish You Take to the County Fair

Know how to tell a real cowboy from a wannabe? Not-so-serious university researchers found that a real cowboy has a horse, a dog, and a pickup truck as his best friends; he thinks a web site is a spider's home and that downloading means getting the cows off the truck and uploading means putting them back on.

Wannabes, on the other hand, think a halter is a skimpy blouse; believe mustangs run best on high octane and think a necktie party is an event to show cowboys the latest trend in fashion.

This clever, laugh-out-loud collection of 165 jokes, anecdotes, and riddles about cowboy life, was written by a collaboration of 15 writers and illustrated by Western cartoonist Jim Willoughby. His cartoons have appeared in *Arizona Highways, Look, Saturday Evening Post, Colliers, Family Circle* and hundreds of other magazines.

Softcover. 144 pages.
#ACWP7 $6.95

Never Give a Heifer a Bum Steer
by Marshall Trimble
illustrations by Jack Graham

Arizona's official historian Marshall Trimble likes the Irish proverb "A smile is a curve that straightens things out." And there's lots to chuckle about in his latest book based on a fictitious population in Ash Fork, Arizona. If the characters in his book were real, the West would have been lost.

Take the Looney brothers. They were advised that the best way to start a cattle ranch — excluding rustling — was to buy a stout bull and fine heifer and let them go forth and multiply. But they were hoodwinked, and the result is summed up in the book's title. Or Doc Pringle. His advice for curing insomnia is to get a good night's sleep.

Preposterous stories, told with a historical perspective and a balladeer's sense of drama and irony, make this book entertaining reading for fans of Western culture.

Softcover. 144 pages.
#ANVP9 $7.95